AVERY
an imprint of Penguin Random House
New York

THE PAIN d'AVIGNON BAKING BOOK

a WAR, an UNLIKELY BAKERY, and a MASTER CLASS in BREAD

ULIKS FEHMIU with Kathleen Hackett

Photography by Ed Anderson · Story illustrations by David Polonsky

AVERY

an imprint of Penguin Random House LLC
penguinrandomhouse.com

Photographs by Ed Anderson
Illustrations on pp. 3, 14, 17, 129, 157, 175, 191,
257, 277, 335, and 339 by Jeffrey Fisher for
Café d'Avignon
Story illustrations on pp. 20–21, 26–27, 32–33,
36–37, 44–45 and 312–313 by David Polonsky
Café d'Avignon branding by Mucca Design

Most Avery books are available at special
quantity discounts for bulk purchase for sales
promotions, premiums, fund-raising, and
educational needs. Special books or book
excerpts also can be created to fit specific
needs. For details, write SpecialMarkets@
penguinrandomhouse.com.

Library of Congress
Cataloging-in-Publication Data
Names: Fehmiu, Uliks, author. | Hackett, Kathleen,
author. | Carbone, Mario, writer of foreword.
Title: The Pain d'Avignon baking book: a war, an unlikely
bakery, and a master class in bread / Uliks Fehmiu with
Kathleen Hackett; foreword by chef Mario Carbone.
Description: [New York]: Avery, an imprint of Penguin
Random House LLC, [2022] | Includes index.
Identifiers: LCCN 2022004400 (print) | LCCN
2022004401 (ebook) | ISBN 9780525536116
(hardcover) | ISBN 9780525536123 (epub)
Subjects: LCSH: Cooking (Bread). | Pastry. | Baking. |
Pain D'Avignon (Bakery) | LCGFT: Cookbooks.
Classification: LCC TX769.F44 2022 (print) | LCC
TX769 (ebook) | DDC 641.81/5—dc23/eng/20220201

Printed in China
10 9 8 7 6 5 4 3 2 1

Book design by Ashley Tucker

For those who left their homes
in search of a better life

CONTENTS

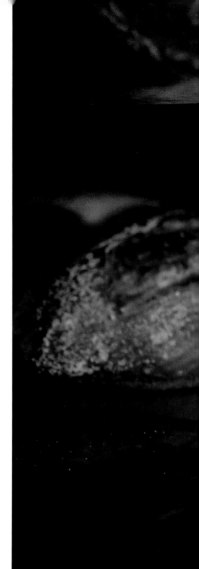

FOREWORD

· · · · · · · · · · · · ·

At certain restaurants, there's a story behind every detail. You can't expect the audience to notice all of the choices, because that's not the point. You just hope that the thought, sweat, and care conspire to make them feel something.

On that note, I'd like to tell you about an unassuming-looking dark bread Pain d'Avignon bakes for The Grill, a restaurant in Manhattan I run with my friends Rich and Jeff.

Five years ago, the three of us got the chance to take charge of the dining rooms at the Seagram Building, the only landmarked restaurant interiors in New York City. It was the biggest moment of our careers. We knew that if The Grill, our new concept for the space, was going to draw inspiration from America's culinary history, we had better do our homework. We spent a year combing through archives and calling on scholars and experts. We drove to antiques shops around the country. We made dishes like venison Cumberland that probably hadn't shown up on a restaurant menu in over fifty years.

After we fine-tuned, we fine-tuned some more. Even the bread basket—a custom that few restaurants embrace nowadays—was a major priority. Specifically, we wanted to re-create the anadama loaf I'd read about on one of those long days at the New York Public Library. A combination of wheat, cornmeal, and molasses, this yeast bread started popping up in New England bakeries around the mid-1800s.

How could we make the best version possible?

Bane at Pain d'Avignon NYC was the only person I considered for the job. He had proven himself to us before, big time, when he developed the sesame roll that is the backbone of our casual red-sauce spot, Parm. That is correct: An Italian American kid from Queens asked a guy from the former Yugoslavia to make the bread for his sandwich shop, and it turned out perfect.

For the anadama, Bane honored the source material while stealthily incorporating a few modern techniques to up its flavor and shelf life. He didn't just replicate a recipe; he nudged a tradition forward. I'll leave it to him, Uliks, and the rest of the Pain d'Avignon team to tell you all about that process in this tremendous book, of which the anadama is only a small part.

With warmth and clarity, they give away all of their knowledge: the techniques behind the croissants, the quiches, the escargots, the baguettes. Everything. As if that weren't enough, they spin one hell of a narrative, about fleeing war, finding a new home, and mastering an ancient craft, all while giving space to the stories of the people who make up the fabric of Pain d'Avignon, many of whom are also immigrants.

The average customer picking up a pastry would probably have no idea about any of this—which brings me back to what I was trying to say at the top.

When a vision resonates, there are probably many more reasons than meet the eye.

Mario Carbone

THE CAST

Branislav (Bane) Stamenković—friends since the age of seven; cofounder of Pain d'Avignon, runs the New York City branch

Vojin Vujošević—friends since the age of eight; cofounder of Pain d'Avignon, runs the Cape Cod branch

Igor Ivanović—met him when he was fourteen; cofounder of Pain d'Avignon, owner of Iggy's Bread in Cambridge, Massachusetts, and Iggy's Down Under in Sydney, Australia

Toma Stamenković—Bane's brother; met him when I met Bane; Pain d'Avignon partner, runs the Cape Cod branch

Teofil (Tole) Zurovac—met him when he was twenty-three; Pain d'Avignon partner, runs the New York City branch

PROLOGUE

An Improbable Journey into Bread Baking

My name is Uliks Fehmiu. The guys on the previous page are my friends and my partners. Former and present. We have known one another for most of our lives, and now they have entrusted me to write a book about the bread that kept us together through the good times and bad.

Pain d'Avignon is an artisanal bakery that started on Cape Cod and expanded to New York City. We baked our first loaf of bread in 1992. At the time, we had no professional training. Not one of us had worked a single day in any other bakery but our own. And yet, now, we provide bread to restaurants with Michelin stars, high-end hotels, and specialty food stores. We are among the pioneers of artisan bread baking in the Northeast.

I've wanted to be an actor since I was five years old, when I first visited my father's movie set in Rome. He was filming a melodrama called *The Last Snow of the Spring*. I was spellbound by the set, the people, the energy, and his beautiful costar, the Italian actress Agostina Belli. It was a new world, a different world that excited me endlessly. Years later, I decided to apply to the Faculty of Dramatic Arts in Belgrade, despite my father being hesitant and warning me of the perils of an actor's life: "You will always depend on others; you will never be your own boss like a painter or a sculptor. In theater and especially in the movies, you are just a color on someone else's palette. Your work? It can be altered over and over again by others," he explained. It was unpredictable. It was unstable. It was not secure. Every time we had this conversation, he would end it with the same anecdote. When he was ten years old, he had apprenticed with a shoemaker. He learned how to stitch the fabric, meld the sole, stretch the leather, and polish the shoe. He knew how to use his hands to *make* something. He had a skill that he could always depend on, a trade that would always support him. No matter the circumstance, he could depend on himself. "If you learn a craft, you will never be hungry," he advised. "Learn to do something with your hands."

I was sure my father had no idea how to make shoes, and that this was one of those exaggerated lectures parents give in an attempt to scare their child away from something. Of course, I did not listen. In 1988, I began attending the Faculty of Dramatic Arts. I eventually became a professional actor and worked alongside my then girlfriend, now wife, Snežana, in theater and film. But, as it turned out, by the early '90s, the world we had always known collapsed. The Yugoslavian War was tearing our home apart. So, Snežana and I decided to leave the country and our careers in protest of the war.

We arrived in a new country that was unknown to us, and where I did not speak the language. Acting could no longer support us. We needed to find a way to survive, and in a strange string of events, I found myself learning how to do something with my hands. Circumstance pushed me to learn the craft of bread making so I wouldn't go hungry. Back then, I saw it as a skill for survival that I could always depend on. I had yet to discover it as an art.

The fact that my friends and I somehow opened a bakery upon arriving in America with no prior knowledge of the craft still surprises people today, but that it all began in as unlikely a place as Cape Cod shocks them even more. What were a bunch of twenty-something kids from Yugoslavia doing baking bread on the Cape? We had zero experience in baking, not to mention in running a business. Necessity, luck, naivete, all played a role.

Our hope is that, despite our unconventional path—or perhaps because of it—you will take advantage of the knowledge we have acquired through trial and error, the generosity of passionate bread bakers, and our own desire to bake the very best loaf of bread.

Ideally, our recipes and techniques will take you confidently on your own bread baking adventure. But let's hope it is less of an odyssey than it was for us and more of a grand tour. The methods we've developed have helped us survive—and thrive—for over twenty-five years. Not only have we learned how to run a business and create something that we are proud of but, most important, we have found our home.

I often walk through our bakery, looking at the breads on the shelves, and wonder, "Is this real? Do we really know how to make bread? Is this an accident?" And then, I close my eyes. I take a loaf in my hands. I squeeze it. The crust is dark and thick and thin and crackly. I rip it apart. I bite into it. The interior is silky and moist. It's so good. I open my eyes. And I no longer wonder.

The last Yugoslavian war ended over twenty years ago, but at the time of this writing, it seems that the nationalism that fueled it was never vanquished. The fear of the "other" is still present and is used by those in power to stay there indefinitely. Instead of nurturing diversity and inclusivity, humanity is heading toward fear of the other and further separation and isolation. We thought that America was immune to this disease, at least internally. I hope we were not wrong.

I'd like to think that a good loaf of bread has the power to bring—and keep—people together, wherever they may be. That is certainly the case for us, now that we call the US our adopted home. Because home is wherever you break—or in our case bake—bread together.

Uliks Fehmiu
New York City, 2021

ACT I

Belgrade—Before the War

I met Bane on the second day of elementary school, when we were seven years old. I remember the day specifically because it was the same day my brother, Hedon, was born. We first encountered each other on the soccer field behind the school, where we were playing on opposing teams. Bane was wearing the coolest sneakers I had ever seen. They were bright blue, orange, and yellow and they stood out against everyone else's identical plain white Shanghai sneakers. Bane had long, silky hair, which was very unusual for a grade-schooler at the time. I fell in love. There is no other way to describe it. We became close but also very competitive on the soccer field. Around the same time, I met his brother Toma, who was three years older. But no sooner had my friendship with Bane cemented than he left with his family to live in Iraq, where his father, a textile executive, had taken a job. I was heartbroken. Bane would visit Belgrade on school breaks for the next five years until, finally, the family returned when he was in the sixth grade, at which point we just continued where we left off. We started smoking together at the age of twelve, went to high school together, and later served a mandatory year in the military at the same station.

Vojin was a year younger than us. He also left the country for a couple of years with his parents and returned around the same time as Bane. We all started hanging out soon after. Vojin was a good-looking kid—he had flawless olive skin, black curls cemented with hair gel, and the profile of a Greek god. The girls loved him. He was also a spoiled brat, and always had everything no one else had at the time: the first VCR player, the first stereo system, the first motorcycle. He was unusually adept at driving stuff, whether it was his motorbike, or his parents' car, which he would steal and take to Zurich for a weekend. He was (and still is) a phenomenal skier. Like fucking Ingemar Stenmark. Vojin was that kid who seemed to have it all together in every realm; he even had an aesthetic sense. He was my second crush. Back then, if you asked me how I would like to look, I would unhesitatingly say, "Like Vojin."

Igor entered the picture in high school, when we were all fourteen. Like Vojin, he was into motorcycles, which gave him an air of cool, despite his nickname, which was Sugar. He cut quite a figure: Atop his tall, skinny frame, a fountain of unbraided dreadlocks sprang from his head. On one occasion, he came to school riding his bike with a rose in his mouth, hoping to impress his crush at the time. When another girl spied him from a second-floor window, she yelled, "Hey, Sugar!" which we all heard. And that was that. Igor always had an aura of responsibility around him. He was the best student among us. On the other hand, he always seemed just a little spaced out, as if he were sleeping with his eyes open. Igor liked to imagine things, to dream about the future.

We were born and raised in a country that does not exist anymore. If you ask me, it was the coolest country on Earth. And in my youthful mind, this is why I sometimes thought then that it had ceased to exist. It was called Yugoslavia.

The former Yugoslavia, in the heart of the Balkan Peninsula, spans a region where Catholicism, Orthodox Christianity, and Islam intersect. It is bordered by Italy, Austria, Hungary, Romania, Bulgaria, Greece, and Albania. To the west, the Adriatic coast and its ports are a gateway to the Mediterranean—and the rest of the world. Surrounded as it is, there is a rich mix of cultures, religions, traditions, and customs. It's where Austro-Hungarian and Oriental architecture clash beautifully. Where one could ski in the Alps in the morning and swim in the Adriatic that afternoon. Where, in the same pastry shop, one could find baklava by way of Turkey or Greece, and Sachertorte compliments of the Viennese. Indeed, the food that we grew up eating swung from lots of fish, vegetables, fresh herbs, olive oil, and wine to goulash, sausages, and the other heavy continental foods of Hungary, Germany, and Austria.

Growing up in such a diverse environment was beautiful. It became very ugly only when the differences we once found so sublime were used to divide us. My memory of life in Yugoslavia is a collage of fragmented pictures and images, but I do remember the aromas and flavors with much more clarity. When I look back on our childhood in Belgrade, here's what I see:

Hole-in-the-wall, white-tiled neighborhood bakeries. When we were kids, our parents would send us to the bakery to buy bread. Some had only a walk-up window, while others had a bar along one wall or the front window where you could stand while having a quick bite. I always had to work up the nerve to peek into the back room where the bakers, hunched over a huge worktable, masterfully stretched phyllo dough with their hands until it was paper thin. I watched in awe.

As teenagers, the bakery was invariably a stop in the early-morning hours after a night of carousing. There was nothing like eating *burek* at 3 a.m. The thin, flaky phyllo dough pie filled with minced meat and onion or cheese always tasted good, but especially

so at that hour. God knows how many sunrises we saw with burek in our hands. There was *kifla*, a croissant-shaped roll made from a semisweet enriched dough and *djevrek*, the sesame-coated Turkish cousin of the bagel. We always, always ate these with drinkable yogurt, thick and plain.

Around the same time that we were indulging our cravings, the state-owned delivery trucks filled with bread were making their rounds to mini-markets around the city. The bread was packed into reusable crates, rather than in huge paper bags the way we do it at Pain d'Avignon. From an environmental point of view, it makes so much more sense. The market manager would unload the warm breads directly onto the store shelves, and return the crates to the truck driver. Needless to say, convenience and expediency were not priorities. How we wish we could deliver our breads like that; it would mitigate so much paper waste, even though we do recycle.

It took us a long time after we arrived in the States to understand why the concept of food made from local ingredients supplied by local farmers and butchers was noteworthy. In Belgrade, this was assumed. It was just the way things were. Everything was seasonal. Our parents made weekly trips to the greenmarket, and, like everyone in Belgrade, they brought home whatever fruits and vegetables were in season.

Every fall, our moms used to pickle different vegetables for the long winter. Peppers, carrots, green tomatoes, and cauliflower. Cabbage, pickled whole, was another staple—if you had a big enough pantry or balcony to store the huge barrels it was packed in. It was served as a winter salad, thinly grated or cut by the chunk, simultaneously tender and crunchy, and seasoned with a little paprika. More commonly, the sour leaves of the cabbage would be used to wrap around a seasoned mix of minced meat, rice, and sautéed onions called *sarma,* the national dish of the region that the Turks left behind.

Almost every household has a pantry where, in addition to all of those pickled vegetables, you are guaranteed to find *ajvar*, a roasted red pepper spread. At the end of every summer, the whole neighborhood was fragrant with roasting peppers. Fruits—most commonly rosehip, strawberries, apricots, and, in some regions, plums—are used to make preserves. Some families make *slatko*, which literally translates to "sweet"—whole seasonal fruits like quince, plums, and sour cherries preserved in a thick sugar syrup infused with citrus. Slatko is brought out for special occasions, usually as part of a festive holiday spread.

Yugoslavia's unique geographic position, nestled as it is between East and West, resulted in wonderfully varied food influences. It is the Mediterranean influence, however, that left an impact on us unlike any of the others. We look back on our summers on the Croatian coast as some of the best of our lives. The food was worlds away from Belgrade's continental cuisine; the Mediterranean climate dictated what we ate.

We spent most summers in Rovinj, a beautiful coastal town in Istria on the Adriatic coast, where there were no sand beaches, but rather rocks and pine trees rimming the water. We stayed in a socialist version of an Airbnb: apartments with rooms to rent. Our days usually started at noon with the first stop always the supermarket for a bit of bread, some tinned pâtés, and a little mortadella. Then we would spend the whole day at the beach, lying in the sun, trying desperately to get our white bodies tanned as fast as possible.

Once or twice a month we were lucky enough to afford a sit-down meal. Fish caught that morning by local fishermen and grilled whole, served with just a drizzle of olive oil and a squeeze of lemon. Simple salads of the freshest tomatoes tossed with greens like arugula and radicchio. Tiny, sweet mussels steamed in a garlicky white wine broth flecked with parsley and breadcrumbs called *buzara*. Octopus, shrimp, branzino—we ate it all. Little did we know that Vojin would carry those Mediterranean cooking influences to another coastal town years later, when he added a restaurant to the very first bakery we opened on Cape Cod.

During our high school and college years, in the mid- to late 1980s, we were completely carefree. We did all of the typical coming-of-age stuff: fell in love with girls; hung out at cafés; played soccer as much as possible; saw movies; listened to AC/DC, Duran Duran, and Queen. Weirdly, it seemed that we were having fun all of the time, despite the political situation enveloping us.

During the Cold War, Yugoslavia was not aligned with either the East or the West; it was never part of the volleying between Washington and Moscow. At the time, Yugoslavian passports were among the most expensive on the black market, since having one eliminated the need for visas to travel to the Soviet Union or the United States. Our neighbors from the Eastern Bloc envied us. For them, we represented a free Western country, and we felt the same. We never felt isolated.

For centuries, our region was a battleground for world powers using our ethnic and religious differences to further their own agendas. It wasn't until after the devastation of the Second World War that we managed to put our differences aside. It was time to align around the same ideas for a better and more humane society with equality regardless of class, race, religious beliefs, ethnicity, or gender. Women had the right to choose, workers' rights were protected, and free universal health care and free education were available to all. Sounds pretty progressive, no?

In 1989, the Berlin Wall finally came down and the Eastern Bloc collapsed. Germany reunited and half of Europe was peacefully liberated from longtime Soviet rule. The Cold War was over and Communism was defeated. And slowly, democratic changes began to take shape in Yugoslavia as well.

Because the country was ruled under a one-party system, which was best described as soft socialism, the transition to democracy was supposed to be much easier for Yugoslavia than for other Eastern European countries. But nothing could have been further from the truth. With the arrival of democracy came an explosive nationalism. A federation of six different states, most with their own ethnic majority, each voted in the first democratic elections for their national representatives regardless of their economic or political program. The political leaders of each national group decided to trade in Yugoslavia to Make Serbia Great Again, Make Croatia Great Again, and on and on.

I was raised to respect all people equally and taught that hate was a fast-spreading virus, the hardest one to contain. In our house, we celebrated both Easter and Ramadan because I am the child of a marriage of mixed ethnicities and religions. My father, Bekim, was an Albanian and nonpracticing Muslim from Kosovo, and my mother, Branka, the daughter of a Catholic father and Orthodox Christian mother, is half Croatian and half Serbian. I am a mix of the three ethnicities that trouble one another the most; not unlike being the child of a Palestinian, a Jew, and a German. I was born and raised in Belgrade, where all of my best friends were Serbian. I always felt Albanian. When I visited Croatia, I felt Serbian because of my Belgrade accent, yet in Kosovo, where I would often visit my father's family during the school breaks, I never felt Albanian enough. I was an ethnic mongrel.

By the late 1980s, the rising nationalism and the hate-mongering of the state-owned media in Serbia were growing more and more vicious. It devastated my father, who was one of the first ethnic Albanian actors to work throughout Yugoslavia. He was also the first Eastern European actor to push aside the Iron Curtain and work in the West. The film that launched his international career, *I Even Met Happy Gypsies*, won the Grand Prix at the Cannes Film Festival in 1967 and was nominated for an Academy Award for best foreign film. My father became a national treasure, beloved for a storied international career that brought him together with legends of the silver screen—actors, directors, and producers—and invited invariable comparisons to Jean-Paul Belmondo and Marlon Brando. The *New York Times* anointed him the "Yugoslav heart-throb." Born in Sarajevo, Bosnia, and raised in Kosovo, he spent most of his adult life in Serbia and had roots and devoted fans in every corner of Yugoslavia.

My father was so stricken by the idea of impending war that he became deeply depressed, so much so that he resigned from the theater altogether. He chose to announce this publicly in an interview in Serbia's oldest and most relevant daily newspaper, *Politika*. The interview was a plea for peace that he hoped someone would hear. Of course, no one did. Such an abrupt end spoke volumes; he gave up the most potent and beautiful tool he possessed—words—in silent protest.

Meanwhile, being onstage was the only thing that excited me. Like many parents who are actors, my father wasn't thrilled with my passion. He brought up every reason he could think of to encourage me to reconsider. I listened, but I had already made up my mind. I was going to be an actor. Plus, I wasn't good at anything else. I was lucky to be accepted to the Faculty of Dramatic Arts, where, incidentally, my parents had met.

During that time, high school graduates had to serve a mandatory military service, either before or after attending college. All of my friends and I decided to serve first and then continue our studies later. Bane and I ended up in the same military base in Sarajevo, while Igor was sent to Vipava, a small town in Slovenia. Vojin, who was a year behind us, spent his final year of high school as an exchange student, studying abroad, in Portland, Oregon.

There was no place like the army to experience just how diverse the country was—and how intense the tensions among the different ethnic groups had become.

I don't know what was worse, the morning exercises in the damp, bitter Sarajevo cold, or army food. Bane and I had different ways of coping. He did every training exercise with a limp cigarette hanging from his mouth. He paid off other soldiers to polish his boots, bartering with them for the contents of the care packages his parents sent. His dad had been transferred to New York City, where American cigarettes, chewing gum, chocolate, sneakers, and shaving cream were in ample supply. I polished my own boots, while Bane had a long line of volunteers ready to polish his in exchange for some of those American goods. There was no skirting the food, though; breakfast was usually a can of sardines and a whole onion, while lunch and dinner would alternate between cabbage or bean soup— the worst versions imaginable. We survived eating cookies and chips from the canteen until Bane was transferred to the military library in downtown Sarajevo and managed to get me a permit to leave the base with him once a month. Then, at least we could head straight to Baš Čaršija, the part of Sarajevo center where an old bazaar used to be, and where all of the best ćevapi (kebab) shops were. We would stuff ourselves with ćevapi every single time, since we knew it would be weeks until we would feast that way again.

While Bane and I found salvation in those monthly ćevapi runs, Igor had put his imagination to good use by figuring out how to rig the camp pay phone in order to make free calls. Everyone called him "The Phone Guy," and his MacGyver-style antics certainly helped him when it came to easing tensions with the Albanians. The Albanian soldiers were able to stay in touch with their relatives, many of whom had fled to Switzerland as the inevitability of war was growing. Igor so desperately wanted to be cut loose from the army that after three months, he feigned psychological issues well enough for the medical team to diagnose him unfit to train. As soon as he was discharged, he headed to New York, where he stayed with Bane's parents and Bane's brother, Toma.

It didn't take long for Igor to find fellow Serbs in New York; they hung out at the Sidewalk Cafe on the Lower East Side. The restaurant served as a de facto town square for Yugoslavian immigrants of the bar scene age. Some of them also happened to work for Eli Zabar, the reigning artisan bread baker in the city at the time. All of them got their jobs through Eli's manager, Milan Ratajac, who was also from Belgrade, and is, by a few degrees of separation, the reason we have Pain d'Avignon today. Milan was like an uncle to every Yugoslavian immigrant in New York, larger than life, with a lion's heart. He considered anyone from his home country to be family, including Igor, whom he hired to deliver bread at Eli's. He helped set us on our path and never asked for anything in return.

Igor loved his job at Zabar's. Back then, artisanal breads were such a novelty that when he made restaurant deliveries, which were often during lunch service, the room would go quiet as he walked through the dining room carrying the huge bags of bread. He was dressed as if he were working the front of the house, clad in black Girbaud jeans and a black turtleneck. Chefs relied on Eli's bread, customers loved it, and critics raved about it. Everyone was happy to see Igor. He was a bread rock star.

As soon as Bane completed his army duty, he joined his family in New York. Vojin and I stayed in Belgrade, and I began my acting studies, loving every minute of it. Hoping to have a way out of the increasingly threatening situation in Belgrade, we managed to get American visas at the embassy in Belgrade. Vojin's parents took stock of the precarious political situation and insisted he go back to the States to continue his studies and not to plan on returning home for a while. When Vojin arrived in New York City, instead of registering for classes, he stayed with Bane in his rented apartment, and together they got themselves a different kind of education. Manhattan's nightlife was irresistible.

I stayed behind in Belgrade even though I hated the idea of being trapped, as I was aware that the war could start any day. But something kept me stupidly optimistic. A few years earlier I watched a live broadcast from Paris of the first ever European Film Academy Awards. And there she was, one of the most beautiful theater and film stars in Yugoslavia, nominated that year as best actress in a leading role. While I was watching her, I had this crazy idea that one day she would be my wife. I decided then and there to stay under only one condition: if I had the opportunity to work with Snežana Bogdanović. As time was running out, I got a call one day asking if I would like to be in a play with Miss Bogdanović. So I stayed. I was driven by passion—for the work and for a woman whom I finally met when I landed my breakout role as Larry in Lanford Wilson's *Burn This*.

At this point, Slovenia and Croatia had responded to the Serbian nationalist movement by proclaiming their independence. It didn't take long for Serbia to announce that it was closing its own borders, marking the start of the four-year-long war.

It was a very claustrophobic, nationalistic time. While we were rehearsing *Burn This*, Vukovar, in Croatia, which was only ninety miles away, was being leveled by the Yugoslav army, controlled by the Serbian government. The right-wing part of the theater management called our act of performing an American play treasonous. One morning at rehearsal, I saw a note on the theater's bulletin board. "How long will these Albanians be soiling our stage?" it read. I was the only Albanian in the theater.

There was no physical conflict yet in Serbia, but the country was crawling with paramilitary and mercenaries. During the play's run, the government passed a law prohibiting all males between the ages of sixteen and sixty-six from leaving the country. One night, during the spring of 1992, in the middle of the show's run, my mother came to the theater and told me not to come home—the military police were looking for me. I slept at a friend's house, and forty-eight hours later I was on a plane to Macedonia. Macedonia at the time had not officially separated yet, so it still had no customs control with Serbia. I was able to flee unnoticed. From there, I landed in New York by way of Zurich. And the journey to Cape Cod began.

ACT II

Cape Cod—During the War

You moved 10,000 miles away, but you didn't leave the neighborhood.

—My father, when I moved to Cape Cod

gor found the location for the first Pain d'Avignon bakery by accident. He'd met his future wife, Ludmilla, at the restaurant where she was waitressing while he was delivering bread for Eli's. Like so many Manhattanites, Ludmilla and Igor managed the city's sweltering summers by escaping them—to Hyannis, Massachusetts, on Cape Cod, where Ludmilla's mother had a weekend house. In the early days of their relationship, the two drove all over the Cape, from Woods Hole to Provincetown, in search of decent bread. Nothing came close to what Eli was baking.

Igor convinced his boss back at Eli's to let him load up his car with whatever bread was left over on Friday afternoons, and he'd take it around to the Cape Cod restaurants and shops for tasting on the weekends. With these amazing breads in hand, he knocked on restaurant doors up and down the Cape—and as far as Boston—offering up Eli's baguettes and sourdoughs for chefs to try. This was early 1990, long before artisanal loaves became easy to find. Of course, the chefs clamored for such soulful bread, which meant that Igor went from stopping by restaurants only on weekends to making three round trips to Boston every week. It didn't take long for him to realize that bread needed to be baked closer to where it was sold, an epiphany that changed the course (whatever *that* was) of all of our lives.

This realization came at the same time that Ludmilla discovered she was pregnant. It was hard to ignore the option of living rent-free on the Cape; Ludmilla's mother's summer house was just sitting there. So when in the fall of 1991, Igor and Ludmilla found a 2,000-square-foot building with a small kitchen in the back, a retail shop up front, and a second-floor loft on Main Street in Hyannis for $326 a month, about the same price as a parking space in Manhattan at the time, their final decision was clear.

To help Igor get started, Vojin, Bane, and I all invested along with Ludmilla's brother. Vojin still had a good chunk of his tuition money, and instead of taking college courses, he went straight to Hyannis to join Igor and Ludmilla to run the bakery. Bane and I were to be silent partners, with no involvement in the day-to-day operation of the bakery. I turned to my parents, as did Bane, for a small loan to join them.

It was January on Cape Cod—with endless gray days and a damp chill that stays in your bones until around June. But it barely mattered to Vojin and Igor; they were spending every waking moment setting up the bakery. That first Cape Cod winter, a stretch of seriously bleak months, was brightened that March by the birth of Tamara, the first of Igor and Ludmilla's four daughters. A new baby, a new business, a new country, and the learning of a new craft; this is where they found themselves in the early months of 1992. Along with Ludmilla and Igor's brother Nikola, who had recently arrived from Belgrade, the active members of the Pain d'Avignon team numbered four.

When I landed at JFK after fleeing from the military police that spring, I was paralyzed by the thought of not knowing when and if I would see Snežana again. Yet, a few days later I got word that I would be able to return to Belgrade—and to Snežana—for my role in *Burn This,* without the threat of being drafted, on the grounds that actors were last in the line of duty.

The war I wasn't going to participate in under any circumstances was spreading like wildfire, yet I flew right back into it on one of the last direct Yugoslavian Airlines flights from New York City to Belgrade. As soon as I landed, I had to report to the local police station. They transferred me to the closest Yugoslav army military base, where I was accused of being a deserter and threatened with being sent to Bosnia on the next truck to fight, despite the permit my producer had secured. Bosnia and Herzegovina was the third republic where the war broke out after Slovenia and Croatia. It was the bloodiest, since Bosnia was the most ethnically diverse, with the majority populations being Bosnian Muslims, Serbs, and Croats. Ethnically dividing Bosnia was like trying to ethnically divide New York City. I managed to avoid being sent to Bosnia that day since the truck had left already. The military police did not come after me again, and I didn't question it.

I continued to act in *Burn This* while the Serbian economy was in free fall. The shelves in the stores were empty; there was a major shortage of basic commodities like flour, sugar, and oil. Of course, the black market was booming. People close to the regime were getting rich overnight smuggling gasoline and cigarettes. Lines in front of the gas stations

were kilometers long; people would wait for days for the gasoline to arrive. I was making the equivalent of about $1 for each performance, while Snežana's salary in the Belgrade Drama Theater was about $10 a month; we were paid in dinars, which would lose 100 percent of their value in the same day if you didn't run to the black market and convert them into German currency. The inflation was astronomical, so we felt lucky if we were able to get a pound of apples and a head of cabbage with our theater salary.

While I was performing in Belgrade, my buddies opened Pain d'Avignon's doors on June 8, 1992. The name of the bakery was inspired by a poster Ludmilla had brought back from the Festival d'Avignon, the summer theater extravaganza in France, where the food culture, especially the bakeries, captivated her.

Igor, along with Vojin, had little trouble signing up clients; in fact, often they would oversell the oven capacity by a long shot. Bane, who joined them to help for the summer, drove from Hyannis to New York City regularly, filling his car with huge wheels of Brie and pâtés to make sandwiches to sell in the bakery.

The demands of starting up should have killed them. But Vojin, Igor, and Bane had a secret weapon in Hamdo, the Bosnian baker Igor had convinced to leave Eli's and join them on the Cape. Hamdo walked around Hyannis with his Czechoslovakian girlfriend on his arm as if he were the mayor. That imperious nature informed everything he did, including his bread baking. His method for mixing dough was part gymnastic routine, part circus act. He would hold a fifty-pound bag of flour under one arm, steady a big bucket of water under his left armpit, and eyeball the amounts of each he added, using his knee as a brake to slow the mixer when he added the flour. Hamdo mixed the bread dough entirely by look and feel—he had no use for recipes. Vojin, Igor, and Nikola became his students, yet he refused to use their names, calling them instead his "cubs." He was a demanding teacher, but in the end, the cubs learned basic bread-baking skills—how to mix, shape, score, and bake. It was the first time any of them saw up close what happens when flour, water, salt, and yeast come together.

While the realities of mixing, proofing, shaping, scoring, baking, and selling bread preoccupied the cubs, Hamdo, who was a Bosnian Muslim, was consumed by something far more sinister. He talked about the atrocities happening back home freely and frequently—so much so that his very presence became a heavy reminder just how close, yet how far, everyone was from the brutal realities of war.

Hamdo grew more and more visibly distressed as it became apparent that the Croatian paramilitary forces were killing his people. We all had friends in every republic, and of course, our own roots grew out of them. But Igor, Vojin, Nikola, and Bane were under so much pressure to pull the bakery business together that politics was far from their minds.

Two weeks after the bakery opened, Hamdo showed up to work and announced that it was not only the Croats killing his people but the Serbs as well. The next morning, just like every other, Bane pulled up to Hamdo's apartment to drive him to the bakery, only to discover that he and his girlfriend had disappeared. The war had become personal; Hamdo just couldn't stomach working with anyone whose government was killing his people. He packed up his dough scrapers, scales, baskets, and trays during the night and caught an early-morning bus back to New York and, we eventually learned, back to Eli Zabar. Hamdo was the first of our colorful bakers, and one of the most influential.

For Igor, Vojin, and Bane, that first summer on Cape Cod was almost as harsh physically as the military exercises Igor escaped just four years earlier. Everyone was feeling the acute pressures of running a business. With no professional bakers, few tools, a couple of beginners at the mixer, and wholesale orders that the oven couldn't handle, the mood was tense. Nikola had a knack for shaping the loaves—Hamdo had taught him—and so he suffered the fate of being awakened in the middle of the night to do just that. Ludmilla would begin packing the breads at midnight, often not finishing up until two or three in the morning, with Tamara in a sling strapped to her back. Everyone was always fearful that every time Ludmilla bent to tuck baguettes into bags, the baby would slide right out. There were no job descriptions, and everyone pitched in wherever they were needed, which was everywhere. The twenty-hour days took on a rhythm of baking, packing, and delivering.

No one was available to tend to the front counter because everyone was busy, so customers adopted the honor system, helping themselves to the bread and leaving cash on the counter. Everyone who could got into the act. Bane's mother came from New York to help out by cooking meals for everyone—and wound up routinely chopping through fifty-pound bags of Spanish onions for the ficelles and focaccias sold in the bakery. Bane's two-year-old nephew was also part of the mix; Vojin brought in a Dalmatian puppy to add to the chaos, all while baby Tamara napped on hundred-pound bags of flour. Bane called it their "hippie community." They even had a VW—a Golf, not the quintessential bus—to make deliveries in. It sported the Pain d'Avignon logo painted in gold letters on the front doors and an interior that the Dalmatian had chewed to bits.

That car got a workout. Each day, at around 5 a.m., Vojin and Bane would begin the drive up Route 6A, a two-lane road choked with cars by as early as 7 a.m., as if they were in a car chase, weaving in and out of traffic to make their deliveries on time. They routinely found their customers waiting by the side of the road, practically inviting them to toss the orders out the window and keep going.

Business boomed. Customers thought Pain d'Avignon bread was worth driving miles for. As summer was coming to a close and Bane's bakery bootcamp was ending, he took

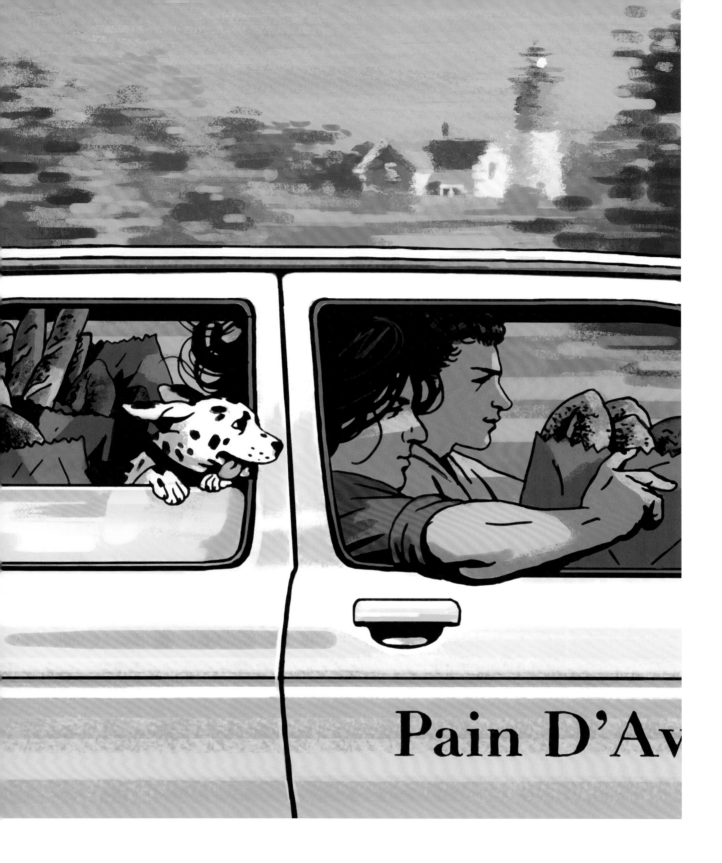

stock of his experience over the three previous months and realized that the business had the potential to grow. He decided to move to the Cape and work in the bakery full time.

Going into business with childhood friends can be harder than being married. Our friendship meant more to all of us than anything—more than money, a job, or a place to live. We lived and breathed our camaraderie. So when Igor and Ludmilla decided they wanted to leave to run their own bakery elsewhere at the end of our first year in business, it tested the bonds of our friendship. We had all been through so much together—displacement, uncertainty, separation, all on top of grueling, twenty-hour days. The split was painful, of course, but looking back, the separation made sense. We were family, and at some point, you have to leave home to figure out who you are. Years later, we would separate once more, providing even more room for each of us to grow. And in the end, by distancing ourselves and our businesses, we were able to help one another immensely.

After Igor and Ludmilla left, Bane's brother Toma, who lived in New York, joined the company as a silent partner. He was the only one at the time who had legal immigration documents.

It was the end of the theater season in 1993, and by then I was performing in all major theaters in Belgrade. *Burn This* was the biggest theater hit at the time, with lines stretching in front of the theater every night and crowds waiting for us after every performance. The atmosphere was more rock concert than theatrical performance. Despite the show's success, the assurance that I would not be drafted to fight a war I didn't believe in didn't last long. When I received a new letter to report for military-reserve exercises in July, I said good-bye to Snežana yet again, got on a bus to Budapest (because the Belgrade airport was closed) with my brother, Hedon, and flew to New York. We went directly to Cape Cod, and from there my brother went to South Carolina, where our relatives lived, and continued high school. It was the summer of 1993, and for me, the beginning of another life.

The days of the hippie community were over; now everyone lived together in a beautiful house on a lake in Hyannis. Each day, I accompanied Bane and Vojin to the bakery, which was located on Main Street at the end of a small alley filled with traditional coastal-town shops. Our arrival turned this quiet alley into a lively and colorful street that resembled a neighborhood in Sicily more than it did a peaceful street in New England. The retail space was small; its counter was covered with baskets full of raisin and seven-grain rolls and big focaccias cut up and sold by the pound. The shelves were filled with baguettes, country breads, and sourdoughs. In the back room, two huge deck ovens shrank the space. I never could figure out how they got them into that room. The space where the dough was mixed was separate from the rest. The floors were covered with black-and-white linoleum tiles in a checkerboard pattern. It was a typical New England house turned into a bakery and a loft.

We inherited Eli's baking practices from Hamdo without understanding completely the reasoning behind them. The bakers who succeeded him had also left their personal imprint on the process. Still, the foundation was there. We knew that in order to make bread, you needed to combine flour with water and add salt and yeast. We called the process of combining these ingredients "mixing." We had two pre-ferments, a sponge (poolish) and a yeasted sourdough starter, which we added to all our doughs. We knew that these pre-ferments were making our breads better, but we really didn't understand how or why. We knew that after the dough had been mixed, it needed to proof, or rise, for a few hours before it was ready to be cut and shaped, and that the yeast was responsible for the fermentation. We understood that heat was responsible for increasing the fermenting activity of the dough and that cold does the opposite. We knew that the breads needed to proof for a second time after being shaped and before being loaded into the oven. We knew that the oven steam made the breads look alive and shiny, and that without it they looked dull and pale.

Since I had no baking skills and my friends likely felt that the work in the bakery was too harsh for me, they gave me a job in the retail store. I ran the cash register, despite not speaking much English at all. I could act in front of hundreds of people, but being behind that counter, unable to communicate, was a kind of stage fright I've never known since.

Looking back, maybe it was for the best, our naivete. That fall, we were paid a visit by the *Boston Globe*'s then food columnist Sheryl Julian. The truth is, we had no idea who she was, not to mention what it meant that she was visiting the bakery. And because Vojin and I didn't have the correct working papers, Bane confided in the photographer she brought with her that we were fearful of being pictured in her story. She laughed it off.

It is hard to describe our shock when we opened the *Boston Globe* magazine on the Sunday before Thanksgiving. Spread across four pages was text and photographs of our breads, as well as photos of Vojin and Bane. We were stunned by the immediate result of the story; customers showed up, clutching the article and asking for the exact breads mentioned. And this lasted for two solid weeks. Our regular customers asked us how it felt to be celebrities, which, of course, was completely lost on us. Looking back, we had no grasp of how lucky we were to get such recognition.

Back home, Snežana was openly and publicly speaking against the war. Surprisingly, she also received a letter to report for military-reserve exercises. No other actress to our knowledge had ever received this kind of a letter. But since Snežana had been able to secure an American visa earlier that year, she packed her bags and left the country. We got married soon after she arrived, and settled on the Cape, and I decided to commit to the bakery.

In the spring of 1995 our daughter, Nika, was born. That same year, the Dayton Peace Agreement was finally signed by Serbian, Croatian, and Bosnian representatives. After three and half years of bloodshed, over 130,000 deaths, and close to 4 million displaced people, this terrible and absolutely unnecessary war was over. Still, the people responsible for starting the war stayed in power. Going back home was not yet an option.

When the time came for Vojin, Bane, and me to loosely determine who would do what jobs, I realized that the only thing I wanted to do was to *really* learn how to make bread. This was the only part of the work that seemed creative to me, and in a strange way I saw a connection between theater and bread making.

I had the good fortune to learn how to bake bread after the bakery had been up and running for more than two years. During those long working hours in the bakery, I couldn't help but think about my father. Here I was, creating something with my hands. In just a few years, his prescient words were beginning to make sense to me. He had another phrase that came into stark relief as I was mixing, shaping, and baking the bread—"Repetitio est mater studiorum," he would say. Repetition is the mother of learning. It was astonishing to me how four ingredients—flour, water, salt, and yeast—could be so humbling. The first time I baked a successful batch of bread it felt good, but I wasn't happy until I was achieving the same results consistently. Slowly I started trusting myself and my instincts. I became mesmerized as I looked through the glass oven door and watched the breads expand as they baked in the oven. Even today, I am hypnotized by the sight. I began to love the process, while Vojin and Bane devoted their time to the business side.

We worked hard, but we always tried to have fun along the way. It is just our nature. Our ability not to look at life too seriously and search for humor in the toughest situations had saved us many times before. To blow off steam—and because we were kids—we would shoot hoops behind the bakery every Friday afternoon, the winner taking all the cash we made from the deliveries that day. It's probably not on the Harvard Business School syllabus, but it seemed like a good idea at the time. Bane drove us crazy because, despite being the smallest among us, he was a sure shot and won almost every single time.

Even so, our breads were getting noticed beyond the Cape and Boston. One of our summer customers from Manhattan loved our cranberry pecan sourdough so much that he brought a loaf to the buyer at Dean & DeLuca, hoping the store might agree to carry it. This was the pre-internet era, and "likes" happened the old-school way, by word of mouth and the telephone. We got the call asking for samples, and before we knew it, we had ten new accounts with a New York City icon and a rented petroleum-blue Pontiac Bonneville for a delivery vehicle. Our daily shuttle to New York—for three months straight—was our way of mixing business and pleasure. New York City was always our dream, but it would be four more years before we had the courage to make the real leap. In the meantime, we remembered what we realized all those years before; bread should be sold close to where it is delivered. When we returned the rental car, the attendant almost fainted when he read the odometer. We put 50,000 miles on that Bonneville.

While we were playing hoops and delivering breads, Igor and Ludmilla were putting down roots in Cambridge. Their mission was more than just baking bread; Ludmilla is an environmentalist to the core (she was recycling long before it became the norm), and very early on Igor started exploring reusable energy. They deeply believe that a sensitivity to the planet—and people—should be at the core of everything they do. When they opened Iggy's Bread of the World in 1994, the response was immediately positive. The combination of their excellent breads and Ludmilla's infectious passion for their socially conscious mission caught the attention not only of customers but of the media; Martha Stewart invited Igor to appear on her widely popular show, and with that, the bakery became nationally recognized.

We were selling to accounts in Boston and so was Igor, and admittedly, Iggy's breads were better. Better looking and better tasting. Each one had character and personality. Even the breads made out of the same ingredients, like raisins and walnuts, or ficelles, looked different and more appetizing when compared to Eli Zabar's original. I wanted to understand why.

Eventually I swallowed my pride and visited Igor at his new bakery for the first time since our separation. He was clearly doing something right. I was duly impressed by the one hundred employee punch cards I counted next to the time clock. He showed me that he was refrigerating the dough once it was shaped into loaves to slow the fermentation—a method known as retarding the dough, which improves the quality of the bread, its flavor, shelf life, and appearance. He had also proudly made the breads strictly with a natural starter and no commercial yeast—the Steve Sullivan (Acme Bread Company) and Dan Leader (Bread Alone) way. Us? We were still using commercial yeast by the boatload, both in our starter and mixed into the doughs. We were making "sourdough" breads, but we actually had no idea what a good sourdough bread should taste like. Learning about the retarding process was a major milestone, but not easy to implement. Igor had huge walk-in refrigerators to cold proof his breads. We had one small walk-in refrigerator already filled with different baking ingredients. But more important, it was discovering that Igor was creating something new. Yes, the ingredients he used were more or less like ours, but the way he was combining them, the way he was fermenting them, allowed him to become not only a producer but a creator. And so, it wasn't until late 1996 that we began the journey to bake the kind of bread that we bake today.

Two huge French baking books, coauthored by a young Éric Kayser, became my bibles, despite the fact that I spoke no French. This was long before Google Translate. My mother, back in Belgrade, was my Google. I faxed pages to her at her theater, where she made copies, had them translated into Serbian by a court-approved translator, and faxed them back to me. My first attempts at using the Kayser methods were not very successful—my breads looked nothing like the pictures in the book—and they were much worse than the breads we were already making. But, for the first time, I started learning about the properties of flour and how it behaves with water, temperature, and time. I slowly began to understand French baking terms, along with the science behind the methods.

I eventually made a natural sourdough starter with water, whole wheat flour, and bread flour and let it do what we still do to this day: sit and refresh, sit and refresh, until it rises and falls predictably. We haven't stopped refreshing that particular starter since. We adjusted all of our existing recipes, used trace amounts of yeast or removed it completely, and reorganized the production. We knew that our hard work had paid off when Boston-based Bread & Circus, the health food and gourmet grocery chain that eventually became Whole Foods, began buying our bread. We caught the wave of the healthy foods revolution in the US without being aware of it. To that end, we spent years explaining to confused customers that the hole in their bread where their jelly dripped through was not a defect but a sign of beautiful natural fermentation.

After almost five years on Cape Cod, Snežana and I started thinking about moving back to the big city. Life on the Cape was beautiful during the summer months—all blue ocean and white sand, and full of energy from the summer crowd. But once September came, blue gradually turned to gray, and the exodus of summer people left us sad and lonely. This emptiness had originally brought us peace, since it was in direct contrast to the turbulent and chaotic environment we had left back home. But as our lives were slowly settling in, we started to miss the vibrancy of a metropolis. We also felt an urge to be closer to film and theater. We needed a change, and Pain d'Avignon was ready to expand.

ACT III

New York—After the War

Bane started talking about opening a business in New York with Tole, a friend he and Vojin had met when they first arrived in New York City on one of their (many) debauched nights that inevitably ended at Sidewalk, the same café where Igor met Milan from Eli's. When we met Tole, it was as if we had known him our whole lives. He was a skinny, long-haired rock and roller who had a great vibe about him. He is that same bundle of positive energy and joy today. It always feels good to be in his presence. He is wise, modest, humble, and very hard-working. At the time, Tole was driving a bread delivery van for Eli's bakery. Tole's wife, Sandra, was working very hard in retail, and they had saved enough money to invest in something of their own. So, it was fortuitous when a Long Island investor became interested in us.

In 1999, while I was trying to figure out how to move to New York City, we were approached by Timothy John, a hilarious, charming, and energetic Lebanese American who owned a specialty foods store in Brattleboro, Vermont, and his business partner and real estate developer, Harvey Auerbach. They were opening a replica of the Vermont store in Water Mill on Long Island's East End. According to Timothy, Harvey was richer than Croesus, which was confirmed on his arrival by private jet at the Hyannis airport, right down the street from the bakery. Contrary to Timothy, who could not stop talking, Harvey was a soft-spoken man with gentle blue eyes. He so loved the Vermont store that he wanted to re-create it in a strip mall in the Hamptons and feature Pain d'Avignon as the in-house bakery. We accepted an invitation to visit Long Island to get a feel for the place, and it only took checking out the price of breads in the area's supermarkets to sell us on the idea. Customers paid twice as much for bread there as they did on the Cape. So why not tempt fate, invest every penny we had, and take yet another chance? Opening a bakery in New York City was always the dream. So, when we were offered the chance to

open a small bakery inside a gourmet food shop just a quick drive from the city, all we could think about was that it was one step closer.

The plan was for Tole to run the mini bakery, but since he'd never baked a loaf of bread in his life, I needed to teach him. We set up the bakery on the second floor of the building, this time with an appropriately sized refrigerator to ensure a proper cold proofing of the breads. The oven was located on the ground retail floor so we could bake in front of the customers. We fired the oven and started baking about two weeks before the market opened. In no time we had built a respectable business for ourselves and had gone beyond the retail bakery to sell our bread to restaurants throughout the Hamptons. I was going back and forth from the city, and Bane would come from Hyannis on the weekends to help us out. It was so refreshing to make the bread in small quantities; it allowed us to dedicate attention to every detail.

As summer arrived and our opening day approached, our excitement was palpable. We were trying to estimate how much bread we should make for the first day, since we didn't want to run out. We tripled the quantity that we had made the day before for the store, working almost twenty hours straight. When we returned on four hours' sleep, we were not physically or emotionally prepared for what came next. Since we had tripled the amount of bread in the walk-in fridge, the temperature inside it had significantly risen, and almost all the breads were on the verge of over-proofing. I went to the bathroom and cried for a minute or two. When bread is on the verge of over-proofing, any sudden move can cause it to deflate. I had to handle every single loaf as if I were trying to diffuse an explosive device. When a loaf did deflate, I wanted to cry each time. Luckily, we were able to save most of the bread—and it was a hit.

Shortly after the opening of the Vermont Market, it became clear that it wasn't going to make it. Not even a decent prepared-food section could obscure the fact that this was a store built from Vermont barn wood and filled with candles and soaps—in the middle of the Hamptons. To save his mini mall, our landlord wanted to bring in one of the famous New York specialty food stores known for the best and freshest fish in town. The idea was that we would become the exclusive bakers for this high-profile store, but in the end, this arrangement didn't work out. The new store took over the lease, and we eventually settled with them, getting a small percentage of our lease back, just enough to find our own space. We had to start over completely.

Manhattan was too expensive, so we found a space in a warehouse in Long Island City. Bakeries are very often dark, humid, dusty, and hot, but this was a bright and airy space with a lot of windows and light. We would need to do a bit of construction, but in a stroke of luck, our landlord, an old-school city contractor, offered to finance the construction costs, and Bane's father helped us with the equipment financing we needed for the wholesale operation. We purchased a bigger oven and a bigger walk-in refrigerator for retarding the breads. For the first time, at least in our minds, we created almost-perfect baking conditions in order to make the bread of our dreams. We painted the floors green to attract the money and opened our Long Island City bakery on October 16, 2000.

My brother arrived that spring from Belgrade. After coming to the US with me in '93, he returned to Belgrade that same year. He stayed there throughout the war, managed not to be drafted, and finally, after all the wars were over, decided to join us. Initially he worked as a busboy in Manhattan, a job he wasn't really suited for. My brother was a big baby whale with piercing blue eyes—not a really fast-moving individual. His super-fast and skilled coworkers from Latin America gave him the nickname Schumacher, after the legendary German Formula 1 champion. The irony was obvious. Once we were ready to open the bakery, he quit his Formula 1 job and joined us, though he knew absolutely nothing about bread making, of course.

That year, we worked 184 eighteen-hour days without a single day off. Snežana would come during the weekdays to do office work before picking up Nika from kindergarten. Since there were only five of us working in a 5,000-square-foot space, the bakery seemed huge and empty. In order to fill the void, we would blast a new album by the famous Bosnian pop singer Dino Merlin. It was a sentimental, kitschy album, perfect for our optimistic mood at this new beginning.

Our first employee was Mr. Iqbal, who had recently arrived in America from Pakistan and whom we only ever called by his last name. He was an old-fashioned gentleman, very proper and polite, who dyed his hair with henna. The long British rule had left a strong mark on Mr. Iqbal, and he treated us as if we were young British aristocrats, not immigrants from the Balkans. There was always a bit of sadness surrounding Mr. Iqbal: He led a nice middle-class life in Pakistan before something went wrong. His daughter was married and lived in Canada, but he never visited and neither did she. He lived in a studio apartment with six other taxi drivers from Pakistan. They all slept in one bed, three at a time while the other three were on the road. Because he was the last one to join the tenants, he had to sleep at the bottom of the bed. All night long he had to wrestle with cab drivers' feet in his face. His exhaustion pushed him to politely ask if he could sleep at the bakery. There was nothing but a few old desks and chairs there, but Mr. Iqbal had an idea. The long back seat we had removed from our minivan in order to fit in more bread for deliveries was just sitting in a corner of the bakery collecting dust. Wouldn't that make a great bed?

The area of Long Island City where we started our bakery was very different twenty years ago than it is today. During the early-morning hours as we loaded our van, we would often be approached by local prostitutes on their way home. In the ensuing years, more than once, our employees were robbed at gunpoint just a few blocks away from the bakery. So it made sense for someone to be in the bakery at all times. Mr. Iqbal became our guardian angel, a good spirit protecting our little shop. He made our bakery feel like a home. When we arrived to work, no matter what time of the day or night it was, he was there to welcome us. He was like a favorite uncle.

We were not sure if anyone in New York City would want to buy our breads since there were already beautiful breads available from bakeries that we ourselves admired, Sullivan Street and Balthazar among them. In my attempt to bring something new to New York City, I tried to re-create Igor's *pane francese*, the ciabatta-like bread that made him famous (see page 95). With a lot of trial and error, we created a bread that we felt was not an embarrassing attempt to copy something, but a bread that was an ode to Igor's creation. The customers felt the same. Our *francese* and our cranberry pecan were two breads that no other bakery in the city was making, and they opened many doors for us.

Our first phone call was to Dean & DeLuca. Angel, the bread manager we knew from our first foray, was still there and she bought from us right away. In the early '90s, artisanal bread was still considered an exclusive niche, mostly only served at expensive restaurants and hotels or on offer at high-end specialty food stores. Our philosophy was the opposite of this. We believed that good bread should be accessible to every possible consumer. So, we offered our bread at slightly lower prices to our retail customers, who then passed this savings directly to the consumer. We started getting retail accounts without much trouble: Citarella, Zabar's, Fairway, Agata & Valentina, Grace's Marketplace, and Balducci's. Angel loved our breads, and she told the *New York Times* food reporter Florence Fabricant about us, who then wrote: "Take a Serb, Branislav Stamenković; an Albanian, Uliks Fehmiu; and add a Bosnian, Teofil Zurovac, and what you wind up with is great bread."

Bane worked furiously to gain accounts, among them the Peninsula hotel. He loved going to sales calls straight from the bakery, covered in flour. He showed up with a two-page handwritten product list. Chefs and purchasing directors loved him. For his visit to the Peninsula, he brought our usual bread lineup, but their general manager wanted a roll as elegant as a baguette with the same texture and crust, but only two bites in size. The next time Bane went to see him, he brought him an epi baguette, which resembles a branch of wheat. The manager didn't want his staff or the Fifth Avenue ladies to have to break each ear off, however. So I took a pair of scissors and cut the dough all the way through. And that's how the epi roll came to be. To make them, we cut a baguette as it proofs into twelve tear-shaped pieces and then we bake them directly on the hearth. We also started hand-making individual miniature baguettes, a very time-consuming process. But these two new items made us the talk of the town among top New York chefs, and we had the blistered hands from all of that cutting to prove it.

One would think that New York, one of the biggest cities in the world, has a huge, competitive restaurant community. In reality, it's small. Despite being one another's competition, most chefs are great friends—genuinely respecting, appreciating, and inspiring one another. Once we started going from restaurant to restaurant offering our breads, we were fortunate enough to create relationships with some of the most talented chefs of our time. They, in turn, passed our name on to other chef friends. Soon our bread was served at some of the top New York restaurants and hotels: The Waldorf Astoria, The Plaza, Ritz-Carlton, Le Cirque, La Caravelle, Aureole, Town, Cielo, Gotham Bar and Grill, The Modern, La Grenouille, Eleven Madison Park.

Our success was affirming, but I couldn't shake the idea that this bread-making business wasn't really an art. That changed the day I paid a sales call to the Four Seasons Hotel. Everyone was impressed with the breads, but during the meeting I could not help but tell them that I was really not a baker but an actor. When I told Snežana about the appointment, she took my hand and looked me in the eyes. "We have this blessing in our lives, and you don't see it. This type of baking is an art form itself and many chefs who are supporting us are artists themselves. Getting their approval is something that should make you look at your own work differently!" Snežana was at the peak of her beauty and her career when she left Yugoslavia in protest, while I was merely a graduate student with just a few theater and film roles under my belt. She knew that she exchanged the bright lights of the stage for years of the invisibility and silence of an immigrant. Yet, it seemed that she had more courage to accept our new life and walk forward unafraid than I did. It took me a long time to stop seeing ourselves as victims of this terrible war, but she helped me see differently.

With all due respect to my esteemed father, I would agree that baking is a skill, but it has become for me as much an art as is acting. In both endeavors, there's lots of waiting. And no matter how many times I've done a scene or proofed a loaf of bread, I'm never certain it's going to turn out the same way. Practice, practice, practice undoubtedly gets one close to mastery. But most important, it is fulfilling a burning desire to create. What separates us humans from other species is the ability to imagine things. To see things in our mind's eye that don't exist yet but could be created tomorrow. Ever since that conversation, Snežana and I have found a way to create again in theater and film, while continuing to imagine the breads we have yet to make.

After this initial takeoff, we never had to go and look for business again. We grew and expanded on our own terms. In those early years, our salaries were extremely modest, and every dollar we made we reinvested in the bakery in order to make it nicer and make our employees' lives better. Our employees were scheduled to work an average of forty hours per week, never more unless it was absolutely necessary. We knew how hard the life of a baker was, as we'd been doing it for years, and we treated our employees with much-deserved respect and appreciation. Since we grew up in a socialist country where universal health care was available to all, we could not allow the people who worked with us to struggle to pay a doctor. We were a four-year-old company when we offered health care to all our employees at no cost. It was years before Obamacare.

Deep down I think we are in constant search for the tastes and flavors of our childhood. In our last year of high school, we celebrated Igor's birthday in a little village called Buci, a few hundred kilometers south of Belgrade. We stayed at his aunt's house, a typical Serbian home sitting at the very bottom of a mountain called Jastrebac, nestled among vineyards and plum trees. Aunt Angelina grew her own vegetables and made her own wine, plum brandy, and grappa. She baked us bread the old-fashioned way: She dug a hole in the ground and made a fire, and once the fire was out she removed the embers, brushed off the ashes, and placed a loaf of bread in the hole. Then she put a metal dome above it and covered it with the glowing embers. That is the best bread I ever had in my life. I am still trying to re-create it.

So many events in our lives seemed like the end of the road. Yet, when one door slammed in our face, another one would open. It was impossible to be aware of it at the time, and it was only much later that we were able to understand that some of the most traumatic experiences in our lives were leading to something good. The terrible war, youth interrupted, friendship and partnership breakups, many ends and new beginnings taught us one thing: to be patient and to trust the journey. Because the journey itself is the ultimate reward.

GETTING STARTED

Four Ingredients, a Lifetime of Sustenance

Flour + Water + Salt + Time = Bread

Before any meal, while everyone was still gathering around the table and settling down, my father would cut and set aside two thick slices of bread for himself. Only later I realized that he was actually making sure that no one else would take "his" bread, even though there was more than enough bread for everyone. My father was one of eight siblings, all born in the decade preceding and during WWII, and often a single piece of bread was the only meal they had during the day. If he was not fast enough to get the bread, his other siblings would devour it in front of his eyes without mercy. In our household, bread symbolized survival and gratitude. My childhood was of course a happy one, but our relationship with bread was formed silently by our parents, who survived on it alone. Bread was an unavoidable and central part of every meal.

Out of this humbling relationship with bread came a reverence for it that bordered on obsession. In our early, unorthodox education as bakers, it never occurred to us to use inferior ingredients in service to profit. It is cultural as much as it is preference, and it has served us well in the long run.

Flour, water, and salt. All three are essential to a good loaf of bread. Among them, flour is not only the primary ingredient and the source of nutrition, but it is the one most responsible for the integrity of a loaf.

FLOUR

Back home, we took for granted that our wheat came from within one hundred miles of our house, because that's where the wheat fields were. It took us a while to understand that in the States, most people had little awareness of where their food came from, ourselves included. This has changed quite a bit since the early days. We became aware of the negative impact that industrialization and the rules the mass market had on food and the farming industry. We understood the importance of knowing where our ingredients were coming from and how they were processed. Gradually, we began to incorporate locally milled grains into our breads. I encourage you to seek them out, too—at farmers markets, natural foods stores, and, if you're lucky enough to live within range, directly from the miller or from a farmer.

At the very least, use organic flour whenever possible. If it is not available, always use unbromated and unbleached all-purpose flour. In simple terms, bleaching and bromating are treatments of the flour in which chemicals like chlorine gas or potassium bromate are added to improve the texture of baked goods. In truth, it doesn't improve texture—it only makes them uniform. And most important, we want to avoid these additives.

For the recipes in this book, you can use any all-purpose wheat flour with a protein content between 11% and 12%. The protein content determines how the flour behaves once it has been hydrated and transformed into a dough. The protein/gluten level plays a major factor in how much water the flour can absorb, whether the dough will be strong or elastic, and how it will impact the volume of the bread and the structure of the crumb. The higher the protein content, the higher the water absorption rate. High-protein/gluten flours have more strength than their low-protein/-gluten counterparts, and vice versa.

WATER

Like flour, not all water is alike. In general, if you can drink your water, you can use it to make bread. Depending on where you live, your tap water can be on a continuum of soft to hard. Soft water has a low mineral content and can result in slack dough. Hard water, with its high mineral content, yields a tougher dough. If your water yields dough that is slack or tough, you may want to consider bottled water. If your tap water is chlorinated, let it sit out on the counter overnight to allow the chlorine to dissipate or it will inhibit fermentation.

SALT

Any salt used for cooking will do the work, but we prefer sea salt. We use a good-quality fine sea salt in our doughs. It makes sense, given that it is the most naturally derived. Additionally, you should opt for fine rather than coarse salt because it distributes itself much more evenly throughout the dough. Whatever grind you use, be sure you weigh it rather than measure it by volume.

TIME

The most expensive ingredient you'll use in the bread-making process is your own time. Once you get into it, my hunch is that you are going to forget about your other daily responsibilities and focus on this thing that you don't need to do, but you really want to do. It will have a meditative effect, and it will cleanse your brain and your soul. Especially once your hands become active. It takes time to learn a craft and to develop a skill.

In life and in arts, as well as in bread making, simplicity is the key. I honestly believe that a good baker is judged by his or her "naked" bread, one that is free of any additional ingredients, just created with flour, water, salt, and time. When combined, these four simple ingredients can look and taste a thousand different ways. Ultimately, your own taste will make your bread different from any other. The recipes in this book are a mere template we offer to inspire you and to spark your imagination.

Our goal is not to explain the involved science behind the baking process. There are social media videos and the encyclopedic Modernist Bread series, in which a team of over twenty people produced an unprecedented number of pages on the science of baking. Our own journey was quite the opposite. One does not necessarily need to understand the science in order to make a great loaf of bread. When Lionel Poilâne was asked what the key to making good bread is, he said, "One really needs to be in love with bread." We are in love with bread, and we hope you will fall in love with it, too.

BAKER'S PERCENTAGE RATIO AND THE HYDRATION PERCENTAGE RATIO

The term "baker's percentage" refers to how the proportions of ingredients relate to one another in a bread recipe. It is important to think in terms of ratios: The amount of flour is considered 100% and every other ingredient is a percentage of this whole. When people used to ask me how to make bread I would say: "You need a kilo of flour, 650 grams of water, and 25 grams of salt." It is simple as that. Once converted into percentage proportions, these numbers read as follows:

Flour	1,000 grams	100%
Water	650 grams	65%
Salt	25 grams	2.5%

Every bread recipe in this book is based on using 500 grams of flour, so for your purposes, 500 grams of flour is 100%. The recipe will have the exact weight of the ingredients needed, as well as the baker's percentage ratio. The key to understanding the foundation of the bread-making process is understanding baker's percentages. Once you master it, it will become a tool you can use to create your own breads, rather than having to memorize recipes.

Another key is the hydration percentage, which is the amount of water relative to the amount of flour. In the recipe above, the hydration percentage is 65%. This means that water makes up 65% of the total weight of the flour used in the recipe.

Hydration percentage defines three main types of dough:

Firm dough	less than 60% water
Medium dough	60% to 65% water
Soft dough	more than 65% water

The less water present in the dough, the easier it is to handle. If it is drier, it stands to reason that it will stick less to your hands. A higher water percentage requires more skill by a baker to handle properly, since the dough is much softer and tends to stick to everything it touches, including your hands and the surface you work on. On the other hand, the higher water content will give the bread a longer shelf life and many other wonderful attributes. Feel free to reduce the amount of water in the recipe if you find the dough is too sticky and not easy to handle. You will still make great bread, and you will find the process easier to learn. In time you will develop the skills to play with water amounts to your liking.

TEMPERATURE

Ideally, the temperature of your dough should not be too cold or too warm—anywhere between 75° and 80°F—for the dough to predictably develop and grow. The room temperature should preferably be the same. The dough can develop at colder or warmer temperatures, but the time that it will take to ferment will be greatly impacted. If the dough temperature is colder, the fermentation process will take longer, and, conversely, if the dough temperature is warmer, it will ferment faster. During the summer months, when the temperature in our bakery averages over 90°F and all the other ingredients stored in the bakery are likely at a similar temperature, we use chilled water to bring the dough temperature down to control the fermentation. During the winter months, we use warm water to adjust for the cold flour and chillier room temperature. Water is the most direct way to impact the overall temperature of the dough, and it is the one ingredient that can easily be manipulated to achieve what bakers call the base dough temperature (BDT), the sum of the temperatures of the main ingredients used in the recipe. In our case the BDT is 225 to 240°F. The formula below shows how we manipulate the water temperature in order to achieve the desired dough temperature of 75°F:

Room temperature	75°F	90°F	70°F
Flour temperature	75°F	90°F	65°F
Water temperature	75°F	45°F	90°F
Base dough temperature	225°F	225°F	225°F

We call for lukewarm water in all of our recipes, which we have pegged between 75° and 80°F in order to have our doughs bulk ferment between 3 and 4 hours. This long active rest allows the dough to develop complex flavors and aromas. I recommend using an instant-read digital thermometer to determine water and flour temperature. Some bakers find that, after mixing a fair amount of dough, they can determine the temperature just by touching it.

MEASURING

When I first started working in the bakery, I didn't know anything about the alchemy of bread. I compensated by making sure I executed all of the steps involved in mixing the dough as competently as possible. You should do the same. Measuring, or actually scaling, is one of the few steps in bread baking that is entirely under your control. There are so many variables (flour properties, water quality, room temperature, etc.), that you want to execute these steps with maximum accuracy. You will be able to troubleshoot the next steps throughout the process much more easily if the weighing or measuring is done properly.

Weighing the ingredients makes sense because it eliminates the vagaries of measuring by volume. For example, measuring the volume of flour in cups, as opposed to the weight in grams, can yield different results depending on how the flour is handled. An aerated flour takes up more space but weighs less than a more compact one; how you scoop the flour impacts how it fills a cup, and how you level it (if, in fact, you do level it) impacts how much flour goes into the mixture.

It may seem tedious to weigh what might seem like insignificant amounts of salt—why not just call for a pinch?—but the fact is that salts vary in density more wildly than flours. Coarse, flaky, fine—a tablespoon of each of these weighs a different number of grams, so it is necessary to weigh salt, too.

If you are already used to weighing ingredients, you know how much easier it makes the whole baking endeavor. Essentially, you need a good-quality digital kitchen scale—one that measures to one-tenth of a gram is ideal—and a bowl in which to mix the ingredients. There's no need for measuring cups and spoons, and no questioning whether you measured correctly. One hundred grams of flour is 100 grams of flour no matter how you handle it.

In the recipes that follow, we've used metric weight where precision matters: in the bread, viennoiseries, and pastry sections. That said, your kitchen scale does not measure anything below 1 gram, so we've provided teaspoon measures for the tiny amounts of active dry yeast that show up in some recipes. There are recipes that don't necessarily benefit from scale measuring, such as sandwiches, quiche fillings, and cream fillings. These are all written using standard measurements.

Our aim is to make it not only enjoyable to bake an excellent loaf of bread, croissant, scone, quiche, or tart but also to make it a successful endeavor. After twenty-five years of baking, we respect the science and embrace the art, both of which we hope come through in the recipes that follow.

TOOLS AND EQUIPMENT

For the majority of the recipes in this book, you will need metal mixing bowls, a rubber spatula, a digital kitchen scale for weighing the ingredients, an instant-read digital thermometer, a large cutting board as a work surface, a bench scraper, a kitchen towel, a Dutch oven, and parchment paper for baking. For more details on this basic equipment, see the Equipment List (page 338). All additional equipment not listed above will be mentioned in the recipes when it is required. It is also a great idea to have a pen and a paper ready or, even better, a small notebook to write down your observations throughout the bread-making process. Make notes to track the steps: What time did you mix your starter? How long did the dough ferment? What was its temperature? If you compile this data every time you bake, it will help you understand the mechanics of each step and refine your process.

WHERE FLAVOR BEGINS: STARTERS AND PRE-FERMENTS

We call ourselves artisanal bakers; we say that our breads are made the old-fashioned way, using traditional European baking techniques. But what really is the "old way" of making bread? The truth is that the baking process hasn't fundamentally changed in a very long time. As the story goes, it was the ancient Hebrews who discovered the magic of baking dough that had been left out over time. When dough is exposed to air, it ferments, deepening its flavor and turning it slightly sour. The same fermentation process is used in making yogurt, cheese, wine, and many

other foods we consume every day. Understanding and controlling fermentation is probably the most challenging part of the bread-making process. Many master bakers consider this to be the key to making a great loaf of bread, since the quality of the bread largely depends on fermentation.

You already know if you prefer a mild cheese like mozzarella or ricotta, or a strong, sharp cheese like Parmigiano-Reggiano. Cheeses that are mild and gentle are considered "young," which means the fermentation/aging time was not long. Cheeses that are allowed to fully ripen over longer periods, we call "aged."

The same concept applies to dough. Dough, like cheese, is a living thing, and its characteristics depend on its age. This is true both of the bread dough we make and of the pre-ferments—natural sourdough starter, levain, and poolish—we use in making the dough. Young doughs and pre-ferments have a mild and gentle flavor, while old ones, fully matured and at their peak, are more intensely flavored. Since the bread-making process is very intuitive, we use "young" and "old" to help visualize and, more important, "taste" the process even before we begin to understand it.

It is thought that at some point, the ancient Hebrews began adding leftover dough from the previous day to a new batch. This resulted in a bigger, lighter, better-tasting bread that also stayed fresh much longer. When bread ferments, it changes flavor, but it also expands in volume and size. Every day in the bakery we do exactly what the ancient Hebrews did centuries ago. We take part of the batch of dough from the previous day, and we add it to the fresh batch. This pre-fermented piece of dough is called a starter.

How Does Natural Fermentation Begin?

Since I began my baking education midstream, after the bread recipes and the processes at Pain d'Avignon had already been established, I was managing the fermentation without understanding the complex chemical process behind it. I was fortunate to be in a position to observe the process while working on the production line day in and day out.

From the minute that flour and water are combined, the process begins. Add yeast, whether commercial (fresh, active dry, or instant) or wild, and the mixture begins to develop character and flavor. More specifically, once flour and water are combined, an enzyme called amylase, which is naturally present in flour, starts transforming the starch in flour into a simple sugar called maltose. Fermentation occurs when these sugars start to break down and convert into carbon dioxide and alcohol. This transformation process is caused by enzymes contained in yeast called zymase. It is wild yeast, a microorganism present both in air and in flour, that is responsible for the beginning of the natural fermentation process. It is a fairly slow but complex chain reaction, and its activity is impacted by multiple factors: flour quality, temperature, water quantity, length of the fermentation, and more. The same reaction will happen if using commercial yeast, but the fermentation process is much faster. This is because just 1 gram of commercial yeast contains a few million yeast cells, while in 1 kilogram of natural sourdough starter, there are far fewer, only a few hundred thousand. So, breads containing commercial yeast ferment much faster than those made solely with natural sourdough starter.

To put it simply, as yeast eats its way through the simple sugars, it expels ethanol and carbon dioxide (CO_2); it's the CO_2 that makes the dough rise. Over the course of the process—mixing, bulk fermenting, resting, and proofing—the bubbles grow and then inflate even more when the loaf bakes. Lactic acid bacteria, present in the dough, break down the ethanol produced by the yeast into acetic acid, which is just one out of a group of acids that impart the delicate flavors and aromas that make it impossible to stop eating bread.

In the early days, we used a starter made with a fair amount of commercial yeast; it was the quick, efficient way to bake bread. It was also very reliable, reducing the chance of inconsistent loaves. The trade-off is that such speedy fermentation doesn't give the dough time to develop the creamy, nutty, buttery flavors that develop from slower fermentation methods. The slower the fermentation, the longer the yeast has to work its magic on the grains. Commercial yeast speeds up the fermentation, but the result is aerated bread with lackluster flavor.

Once I had a partial grasp of the science, I attempted to make our own natural starter. I knew that Igor was using his own and I had read the Kayser books, but I still had little confidence that it would actually work. I mixed bread flour, whole wheat flour, and lukewarm water. The dough was very firm and dry. It looked completely dead and not promising at all. I put the mixture in a small container, covered it, and let it sit. I constantly visited the room where the container was, but I didn't dare open the lid to take a peek, for fear I might disrupt the process and ruin it. After three days, it was time to open the lid. The dough was not hard anymore, but rather a much more relaxed and softer version of itself. Bubbles had begun to form on the sides of the container and it smelled of pungent cheese. It looked as if it was becoming alive, but I was still not very hopeful.

I pressed on, feeding a portion of the starter (and discarding the rest) with a different pro-portion of bread flour, whole wheat flour, and lukewarm water. I put the lid back on and let it sit for another twenty-four hours. The next morning, I noted how the volume had increased and then collapsed sometime before I opened the lid. I was able to see the marks the dough had left on the walls of the container, the same way you can see how high the sea rose at high tide after it retreats. I repeated the feeding (also called refreshing) and discarding process every morning. My starter was becoming active and I was gaining confidence. I was now not afraid to open the lid and observe it just a few hours after I had mixed it.

As my friend Kathleen would say, natural starters are like infants; they like comfort and consistency in temperature, conditions, and feeding. I used lukewarm water and set the starter aside at a warmish room temperature and was refreshing it every day at the same time. After it had been rising and falling consistently, it was ready to be used to make levain, one of the three pre-ferments/starters we use at the bakery. Our levain is a mixture of the starter with water and bread flour only (no whole wheat flour), which ferments the dough and makes sourdough bread.

Every day, while I was overlooking our regular production, I had a side gig going that looked like a sixth-grade science project. Afraid to take a chance on a big batch of dough, I did trials with smaller amounts until I finally made a bread that I was happy with. The breads were far from perfect—too dense, too sour for my taste, but they had beautiful color and the unmistakable look of naturally leavened bread. The first time I baked a loaf of bread without commercial yeast, I felt like Sir Edmund Hillary must have felt as he summited Mount Everest. I learned some of the most valuable lessons by playing around with the proportion of flour, water, and levain. Once I felt I'd found the right balance, I was ready to take the next step: making the sourdough with no backup plan.

I took the leap and mixed the levain into 500 pounds of dough and . . . it worked. That first batch of sourdough came out of the oven tasting faintly sour, slightly smaller than the breads we made with commercial fresh yeast, but much lighter than my earlier attempts. The loaves were still somewhat dense but with a beautiful creamy crumb and those irregular air pockets, a sign of long and proper fermentation. In other words, they exhibited most of the characteristics of French peasant-style bread.

The improvement in taste, crumb, crust, color—the results of the lengthy fermentation— all but made up for the convenience that using so much commercial yeast had allowed us. We adjusted our production schedule, reduced the amount of yeast in the breads to the bare minimum, and, in some of the breads, completely. When we opened our New York location, we did not start with a new starter; we brought the one from Cape Cod.

We have been using the same starter I developed more than twenty-five years ago to make levain, the pre-ferment that gives our sourdoughs their distinct flavor. Pre-ferments, like doughs, vary in their hydration percentages. They range from the very dry ones at about 50% hydration to the liquid ones that are at 100% hydration. We settled for the one that was close to the consistency of the regular bread dough at 62.5% hydration. In baking terms this would be considered a solid levain. This allows us to play with the percentages of the levain in the final dough without worrying that it will dramatically change its water content.

You can play with amounts of levain according to your own taste. Besides being an important fermenting agent, your starter will impact the flavor of your bread in a major way. In this way, you can think of it as any other ingredient used in the recipe. The amounts of levain in this book range from 15% to 50% of the total flour weight. In the recipes with a higher levain percentage, its presence will be more noticeable, giving the bread a unique aged, smoky aroma when baked.

In the recipes where we use less levain, we allow the grains used to make the dough to ferment without the overpowering flavor of levain. These breads will taste more like the flours used in them, rather than of the levain, which is true for all of our sourdoughs.

How to Make a Natural Sourdough Starter

The minute you combine flour and water, the wild yeast and (good) bacteria from the air, your hands, and the grains in the flour start the fermentation process. This is the first step in making a viable culture for your starter. I recommend using a 1-quart lidded, transparent container to mix it in. You want to be able to see the bubble formations along the walls of the container as the starter begins to ferment.

NATURAL SOURDOUCH STARTER

INGREDIENT	BAKER'S PERCENTACE	WEIGHT (CRAMS)
Lukewarm water (75°F)	62.5%	75 grams
Bread flour	60%	72 grams
Whole wheat flour	40%	48 grams

Pour the warm water, followed by the flours, into the container. Mix with a rubber spatula to incorporate the water into the flours until it forms a firm dough. Scrape the sides of the container to pick up any loose dry particles. Once the dough is formed, finish kneading it with your hands until it feels as though it is one cohesive mass. When all of the flour is absorbed and no dry clumps remain, cover with the lid and set aside at room temperature (75°F) in a draft-free place for 3 days. Over the course of that time, the mixture should relax and come alive, with tiny bubbles forming around the edges and on the surface. If the starter looks exactly as it did when you began or does not begin bubbling, let it sit another day or two until it does. It should smell pungent and sharply acidic. (If a skin forms on the surface, simply peel it back to observe it.)

Feeding Your Starter

Once your starter has bubbles and that funky aroma (which means it is fermenting), it is a sign that it wants to be fed. In the case of our starter, this is roughly every 24 hours. The more consistency—in ingredients, timing, and temperature—the happier and more compliant your starter will be. When any one of these variables changes, the starter will behave differently, and as a result, its appearance, aroma, and flavor will change, too. From the time you mix the flour and water, the dough starts to expand (thanks to that wild yeast). It will grow up to a certain point and then slowly begin to deflate, leaving traces of starter around the edge of the container and sinking a bit in the middle. The longer it sits after it deflates, the more sour it becomes. It helps to be a keen observer; watch for that all-important rhythm of rising and falling.

We prefer a starter that isn't too acidic yet has strength and potency. Let's say it's more like a young pecorino than Parmigiano-Reggiano—it has lots of character and is pleasantly pungent. The idea is to impart strength to the levain and, in turn, to the dough without overpowering it with acidity.

If you plan to begin making bread in the morning (to be baked later that day), your feeding should be scheduled for the morning. It is important that your refreshing schedule be accurate and on time, but all is not lost if you are off by an hour or two on either side of the prime feeding time. Feed the starter in a vessel the same size as the one you built it in.

TO FEED YOUR STARTER

INGREDIENT	BAKER'S PERCENTAGE	WEIGHT (GRAMS)
Natural sourdough starter	10%	12 grams
Lukewarm water (75°F)	62.5%	75 grams
Bread flour	90%	108 grams
Whole wheat flour	10%	12 grams

Place the starter in a 1-quart transparent container. (Discard the remaining starter.) Add the water and squeeze the starter with your hands until it is mostly dispersed in the water. Add both flours and mix using a rubber spatula until all of the flour is absorbed. Rotate the container as you mix the dough, scraping the sides and corners to pick up loose dry particles. Finish kneading with your hands until the flour is thoroughly incorporated. The dough will be pliable but somewhat stiff. Cover with the lid and store at room temperature (75°F).

Every 24 hours for the next 2 to 3 days, feed the starter using the quantities in the chart above: First weigh 12 grams of the starter (discarding the rest) and mix, as above, with the water and flours. Pay attention to how it behaves; in the beginning, it will rise as the yeast and bacteria come into balance, then it will begin to deflate once this is achieved. Once your starter is consistently rising and falling, it is ready to be used to feed your Levain (page 68).

Levain

Levain is made by taking a portion of the natural sourdough starter and mixing it with more flour and water, then allowing the wild yeast and lactic acid bacteria to do their work.

Make the levain 10 to 12 hours before you plan to mix your dough (generally the night before).

INGREDIENT	BAKER'S PERCENTAGE	WEIGHT (GRAMS)
Lukewarm water (75°F)	62.5%	75 grams
Natural sourdough starter	10%	12 grams
Bread flour	100%	120 grams

In a 1-quart container, combine the water and starter until it partially dissolves in the water. When there are just small clumps of starter remaining, add the flour and mix using a rubber spatula, then finish kneading with your hands until all of the flour is absorbed.

When all of the flour is absorbed and no dry clumps remain, cover with a lid and leave it at cool room temperature (about 65°F) overnight. If the air temperature is very warm or your schedule will not permit you to mix your dough 10 to 12 hours after the levain ferments, you can leave it in a warmer place, 72° to 78°F, for 2 hours to allow the process of fermentation to start, then store it in the refrigerator overnight to be used the next morning.

If your levain has behaved well, it should appear alive and bubbly and smell subtly tangy but sweet, unlike the pungent starter. If it smells a bit sour, you can still use it; your bread will just taste more sour (which you may find preferable). If that's not to your liking, combine half of the levain with 75 grams of lukewarm water (75°F) and 120 grams of all-purpose flour and mix as above. Cover and set aside as above to let it ferment until it passes the Float Test (see below) in 2 to 3 hours.

THE FLOAT TEST

Pull a half dollar–size piece of levain or bulk fermented dough off of your batch and gently drop it into cold water. If it floats, it is ready to make your bread rise. If it sinks, cover it and set it aside at room temperature, testing it every hour or so until it passes the test.

Taking a vacation from feeding your starter without starving it is possible; feed it on schedule, then cover and refrigerate it for 2 or 3 days. To bring it back to life, refresh it as above, 2 to 3 days before using.

BREAD MAKING, AN OVERVIEW

MIXING THE DOUGH

It is very important to measure, or "scale," all the ingredients correctly, since it will be very hard, if not impossible, to reverse the effect after this point if you make a mistake or forget one of the ingredients. Write down the recipe in a notebook and make a check next to every ingredient you measure and add to your mixing bowl. Always add the ingredients in the same order.

With most of our breads we use the double hydration method called *bassinage*, a French baking term that simply means that the water is added at two different stages during the mixing of the dough. The first addition (listed as water in the recipe chart) is enough to hydrate the flour so that the gluten can begin to develop; at high hydration levels, gluten develops more slowly. Once it is on its way, the remaining water (listed as bassinage) is added. Gluten is a group of proteins that develops the elastic structure of the dough when wheat flour is mixed with water. The gluten is what allows the dough to be stretched repeatedly without tearing; all that stretching and folding are what give the dough its structure and strength to trap the air that's trying to escape.

Finding the balance between the dough's strength and its elasticity is the baker's goal. The dough needs to be strong enough to resist bursting and tearing as the carbon dioxide gradually builds up during fermentation, yet elastic enough to easily expand to make room for that carbon dioxide. It's like most humans—it needs structure, but it also needs freedom to grow. Stretching and folding make the dough strong; resting it makes it elastic.

The more tactile you are with dough, the better you will become at determining whether the flour has been properly hydrated. The more you bake bread, the better you will be able to determine if all the ingredients are evenly mixed simply by feeling it.

In the beginning, you will want to write down the temperature of the water you used so that you can adjust it accordingly the next time you make the dough. With some practice and attention, your hands will become your thermometer; they will tell you if the dough is too warm or too cold.

For all of our breads, after the initial mixing of ingredients, we let the dough rest for 30 minutes. This step is known as an autolyse, which is a scientific term for the work that the enzymes in flour do when it is combined with water. After we mix the flour and water, along with the pre-ferment, we set the dough aside to allow it to develop passively, which, in turn, shortens the mixing time. This "rest" period of 30 minutes increases the dough's ability to stretch, a sign that the gluten has developed properly.

Bulk Fermentation

As soon as you finish mixing the dough, bulk fermentation begins. Bulk fermentation is essentially the first rise of the dough, when it is fermenting in one piece (the "bulk"), as opposed to later in the process, when the dough proofs (rises) after it has been cut, divided, scaled, and shaped. You do not want to rush the bulk fermentation, as this stage is crucial to the development of the dough's strength, flavor, and structure. With most of the recipes in this book, the bulk fermentation lasts between 3 and 4 hours if the dough and the room temperature are at 75° to 80°F. If the dough or the room temperature is colder, this first rise will last longer; if the dough is warmer, the dough will ferment faster and the time of the first rise will be shorter. Temperature is a major factor, but it is one of only several that can affect the fermentation activity and time. The type, quality, and the freshness of your flour, the quality of the water, and the readiness of your pre-ferment—all of this can affect this first rise significantly. So rather than simply following the proposed timeline, please observe your dough and see what physical changes it goes through.

As the dough is resting, the yeast eats the simple sugars present in the flour and releases carbon dioxide, causing the dough to expand and swell. In the first half of the bulk fermentation, you will not notice much of this expansion in volume. It will be much more visible in the second half of this first rise.

During the bulk fermentation, the gluten strands start to organize themselves, and the acid that is created as the dough ferments gives the gluten strength. In doughs that have a higher hydration percentage and are mixed by hand, our goal is to create a gluten structure sturdy enough to withstand the expansion of gas produced but not so sturdy that it won't allow those gas bubbles to expand. To achieve this, we must perform a series of folds during the first rise followed by resting periods between the folds.

It is an exercise similar to yoga—a constant process of strengthening while stretching and relaxing your muscles. You don't want your dough to be strong like a body builder; you want it to be more like an Olympic gymnast. You want extendibility along with that structure. Stretching and folding also help to even out the dough's temperature, since the core of the dough is always the least affected by the outside temperature.

Record the folding times in your notebook. The folding sequencing and the length of the resting times between them will vary from recipe to recipe. But as a general rule, you will notice that with every fold the dough becomes stronger as it becomes less elastic. It will start holding on to its shape for a longer period of time. The folding and stretching can be more vigorous in the beginning of the first rise. As the dough rises and expands under the pressure of the gas further in the process, you will need to stretch it and fold it more gently in order to preserve the precious gas produced during the fermentation. Once the dough becomes too resistant, it is telling you to leave it alone. If the dough protests, let it rest.

Pre-Shaping

Once the bulk fermentation is completed, it is time to portion, or divide, and pre-shape the dough. The recipes that follow, unless otherwise noted, make two small or one large loaf. Of course, if you are making a single loaf, there will be no dividing.

A metal bench scraper is our tool of choice for dividing and pre-shaping the dough. It makes clean, thorough cuts, and it is also an ideal tool for handling the dough at this stage.

Pre-shaping is meant to give structure to the dough while creating a more uniform shape to work with later on. Pre-shaping is also like a rehearsal for the ultimate shaping of the dough. Because you will directly handle it, you will have a chance to determine how strong it is and how well it has developed during the fermentation process. If the dough feels a bit too loose, pre-shape it with a bit of intensity. If it feels sturdy, go easier on it at this stage.

Shaping

No matter which shape of bread you are making, the basic steps of the shaping process are always the same. At this point, you are already familiar with it, because you have pre-shaped the dough. It is a series of stretches and folds performed to achieve the same goal—to build more structure into the dough and also, at this stage, to give the dough its final desired shape. The final shaping requires a combination of flattening, stretching, and folding the dough onto itself, then shaping it into a round or elongated loaf. Handling the dough with a minimal number of moves is essential.

Regardless of which bread you are shaping, a 1-kilogram round loaf or a brioche bun, the basic steps are always the same. If you want your bread to have an open crumb filled with irregular air pockets, you should shape your bread gently while trying to preserve its structure, and de-gas it as little as possible. When you are shaping breads to have a uniform crumb—most of the breads with fruits and nuts or the ones you will bake in a pan—you should shape it with more force and without fear of de-gassing the dough.

Final Proofing

Proofing is the baker's term for the final rising of the dough after it has been shaped.

As the fermentation process continues, the loaf will continue to swell and develop more flavor. Making sure that your loaf is properly proofed is not easy to determine. This is a skill that gets easier over time. The dough should look and feel aerated, gaining in size and volume, but it should still feel somewhat strong and structured. There is a moment in this process when the loaf reaches its ultimate proofing capacity. Since most of our breads proof at normal room temperature, or in the refrigerator overnight, the window of time when the loaf reaches its proofing peak lasts 30 to 45 minutes. If you let the loaf proof beyond this window, it will deflate as a balloon does and ultimately collapse once you score it (opposite). The bread will lose its structure and turn into a flat disc, the cuts will not open, and it will be pale in color and taste too sour. If the loaf has not proofed long enough, it will "explode" in the oven since the gas has not had the time it needs to settle uniformly throughout the loaf and will seek to escape in an uncontrolled manner through the weakest part of the bread. It will not fully rise in the oven and it will stay small and dense. When the bread is properly proofed, it will look aerated, you will be able to score it without fear of deflating it, it will have a nice oven spring (that final burst of rising just after the bread is put in the oven), its cuts will open nicely, and the bread will reach its full volume. When baked, its crumb will be light and airy, and its crust will be beautifully caramelized with a deep brown sheen.

THE FINGERTIP TEST

The most common way of checking if the dough is properly proofed is to gently push your fingertip into it. If the dough bounces back within 2 to 3 seconds yet still leaves a slight impression, it is ready to be baked. If it immediately bounces back, the dough is not relaxed enough; let it rest for another 30 minutes. If the fingerprint remains imprinted in the dough, it is over-proofed.

In this book we offer guidelines for proofing at normal room temperature (75° to 80°F) for 3 to 5 hours or, as we do in the bakery, in the refrigerator overnight for up to 15 hours. The overnight cold final rise gives you the flexibility to bake the bread when you want. This prolonged fermentation will allow your loaf to develop an even deeper flavor and a blistery crust. Depending on how much the loaf rose in the refrigerator overnight, you might need to finish proofing it at room temperature. If the loaf looks ready—it looks and feels aerated, has gained in size and volume, and feels somewhat strong and structured—you can bake it right away. If it still looks somewhat small and firm, cover it with a kitchen towel and let it continue proofing at 75°F away from any draft. If neither the 3- to 5-hour window or overnight proofing suits, there is an alternative if you happen to have a place to proof the loaves that is 50° to 60°F. At that temperature, the loaves will be ready to bake in 8 to 10 hours.

Scoring

Scoring, or cutting into the surface of the dough, allows it to expand by releasing steam and carbon dioxide during baking. A razor-sharp tool such as a lame or a single-edge razor blade is the best choice for making clean cuts. Acting decisively is also essential. The initial contact between blade and dough sets the path the score will take; try to score assertively or the dough will stick to the blade and the cuts will not penetrate the surface. To make sure your bread will have conspicuous "ears" (these are the overhangs that result from the bloom, when in the oven the crust opens where the slashes are made—the ones you are tempted to tear off when you get your hands on a loaf of bread), hold the blade at a 45-degree angle and err on the side of shallow cuts. That said, cuts that are too shallow—and/or are made at a 90-degree angle—will heal and seal themselves quickly and won't allow the steam to release. The steam has to go somewhere, and with no outlet it finds the weakest point in the dough and bursts right through it. On the other hand, cuts that are too deep can deflate the dough. When working with softer doughs, some bakers put the shaped loaves in the refrigerator not only to slow fermentation, but to achieve cleaner cuts when scoring.

Baking

The deck ovens we use at the bakery are equipped with steam injectors that fill the chamber automatically, creating the all-important humidity that prevents the crust from forming too early and allows the heat to do its job to promote a final flurry of yeast activity so that the bread fully rises. The steam also helps to give breads their burnished crusts. To approximate this sealed environment in a home kitchen, use a cast-iron combo cooker (page 339), a Dutch oven, and for long loaves, a Challenger bread pan (page 339).

We bake our breads at 500°F, until the crust is crisp, thick, and very dark brown, or *bien cuit*. This is a degree of doneness in which the crust takes on a depth of flavor that can be achieved only when its proteins and sugars are exposed to heat long enough to turn the crust so dark. You may prefer yours less so, perhaps golden all over, which yields a thinner crust. A properly baked loaf will feel light in your hand relative to its size, and if you tap it on the bottom, you should hear a hollow sound; this means that the excess moisture has been baked out.

Cooling

It's understandable to want to tear into bread just out of the oven. It's almost unnatural *not* to. But you may know from experience that the texture of hot bread can be doughy, as if it hasn't had time to "set." That's because, although most of the moisture has been baked out (thus the hollow sound when tapping the bottom), the starch granules still contain some moisture that evaporates as the bread cools.

Storing

Sourdoughs made with levain tend to remain fresher longer than those made with commercial yeast for the simple reason that they have a higher level of acidity, which delays mold growth. The truth is, sourdough eaten on the day it is baked will taste different than it will two days later. Some find it even more to their liking then, as the flavor tends to deepen as it ages. Whatever the case, there are ways to store it that will prolong your enjoyment of that hard-won home-baked loaf.

MAKING BREAD, STEP-BY-STEP

1. Mix the Dough

Mixing the dough is a fairly straightforward process, but there are details involved in combining the ingredients that make a difference. You will want to scale the small ingredients like salt and yeast, if using, first and set them aside. Set your mixing bowl on the scale and zero it out. Fill a pitcher with water that is between 75° and 80°F and write down its temperature. Measure the water as directed in the recipe (the water is added in two parts; in the recipe charts the first addition is referred to as water, the second as bassinage), followed by the pre-ferment, and then dissolve it by squeezing it through your fingers. When there are no large clumps of pre-ferment left in the bowl, add any liquid ingredient or sweetener—honey, milk, eggs, maple syrup, or any kind of sugar—that the recipe calls for. Then slowly add the flour to the bowl.

If you don't like working with sticky hands, use a rubber spatula to initially combine the ingredients. Place a small bowl of water near your mixing bowl. Before handling the dough, wet one hand—your mixing hand—lightly to prevent the dough from sticking to it. Keep the other hand clean and dry and available for turning on the faucet or grabbing hold of the bowl. Once the dough begins to form, continue kneading it in the bowl until no dry particles of flour remain in the dough or at the bottom of the bowl. The whole process should not take longer than 5 minutes. Check the dough temperature with your digital thermometer. If your room temperature and the ingredients are all 75°F, the dough should be between 75° and 80°F because the dough

heats up slightly during the kneading process. If it's warmer than that, put it in the fridge for 5 minutes; if it is colder, put it in a warmer room or turn on your oven for a few minutes and set the bowl on top of the stove just long enough to get the temperature up by a few degrees.

Place the yeast and salt in discrete places on the dough surface (do not let them overlap), cover the bowl with a kitchen towel, and set aside in a draft-free place at room temperature (75°F) to rest for 30 minutes.

During this autolyse, the salt will hydrate and become easier to incorporate evenly into the dough. After 30 minutes, add the remaining water (bassinage), if required, and mix as above, until the water is completely absorbed and the salt is distributed throughout. This is also the time when you should add any dry ingredients if the recipe calls for them: nuts, seeds, dried fruits, olives, etc. While you are adding water, the dough will start to come apart. Don't worry. It will come back together to form a cohesive mass as you work it. Continue working the dough until it no longer sticks to the sides of the bowl. Cover it with a kitchen towel and set it aside to rest in that same draft-free place at room temperature (75° to 80°F).

THE WINDOWPANE TEST

One of the simplest ways to determine whether your dough has developed a strong gluten structure is to pull a half dollar–size piece from the batch and stretch it into a thin membrane. If it breaks, it means the gluten network is not strong enough to allow for elasticity. Let it rest for 15 to 30 minutes more and test it again. This allows the dough to expand, making it easier to stretch. If it remains intact but you can stretch it thin enough to see through it, the dough has developed the proper gluten structure.

2. Bulk Ferment, Stretch, and Fold

Bulk fermentation varies depending on the recipe, where the total bulk fermentation time and number of folds will be indicated. After 30 to 60 minutes depending on the recipe, uncover the dough and notice how it has transformed. You will see that the dough has relaxed and spread evenly in the mixing bowl. You will also notice that it has become somewhat smooth and shiny. If you pull it and try to stretch it, you will notice that it is very elastic and doesn't resist too much. At this stage, you want to maintain that elasticity and strengthen the dough at the same time. Stretching and folding strengthen the dough exponentially.

To stretch and fold the dough (see photos): Pull a portion of the dough from the side of the bowl and stretch it upward as far as you can without breaking or tearing it from the bulk. Fold it back onto itself, then repeat this four or five times, working your way around the bowl with each fold. To determine if your dough is ready to be cut and shaped, perform the Float Test (page 68) after the final fold and rest.

3. Divide and Pre-Shape

Use a plastic scraper to separate the dough from the edge of the bowl and gently coax it onto a clean work surface. Try to release the dough from the bowl without letting it fold onto itself. If it does, use your scraper to pry it apart. If making two smaller loaves, divide the dough in half (see below) before pre-shaping. To simplify the process, in this book we pre-shape the dough for all the breads into round balls, with the exception of Pane Francese (page 95) and Ciabatta (page 139).

To divide the dough to make two small loaves: First wet your hands lightly (you will be handling the dough and it will be sticky) and using a metal bench scraper, cut the dough into two equal halves, eyeballing it as best you can. It is not a big deal if one half is slightly bigger than the other. If you prefer to be more exacting, weigh each on a digital scale. As you cut the dough, it will stick to the scraper as well as to the work surface, so use your wet hand as your guiding hand to prevent sticking.

To pre-shape a single loaf: The dough will stick just enough to the clean work surface to anchor itself to it, which helps create all-important tension on the surface of the dough as you pre-shape it. Hold the bench scraper just underneath the dough at 10 o'clock and make deliberate movements to 3 o'clock, guiding and shaping the dough clockwise into a round with your free hand. The surface of the dough will begin to tighten and become smooth and round. After four or five rotations, the surface tension should be ideal. If the surface breaks, it means that you went a bit too far. Don't worry, just stop shaping it. The dough will heal itself and come together again as it rests. Set it on a large clean cutting board and repeat with the second piece of dough, spacing them apart to prevent them from sticking to each other as they expand. Dust the doughs with a little flour, cover with a kitchen towel to protect them from drafts, and let rest at room temperature (75°F) for 20 minutes. (If the dough is very wet and sticky, let it rest uncovered; its surface will dry just a little bit, which makes the shaping somewhat easier.) This short break is known as a bench rest. After 20 minutes the dough should look relaxed; it will have grown in diameter and gained more volume, while maintaining its shape and structure. If the dough didn't spread much and appears tight, let it sit on the board for another 20 minutes to allow the gluten to relax.

If the round of dough begins to lose its structure and spreads out like a pancake within the first 20 minutes after pre-shaping, it is a sign that the dough hasn't fermented enough and needs strengthening. Reshape it as above to give it more structure and set it on the board again, then check on it in 20 minutes. Repeat this step until the dough maintains the desired shape.

4. Shape a Loaf

Remove the kitchen towel and dust the loaf/loaves with a little flour. Because the dough rested on a clean board (no flour) it will stick; use a bench scraper to remove the loaf/loaves. To transfer the loaf/loaves to a clean work surface, slide the bench scraper underneath decisively but gently, taking care not to deflate the dough. Flip the dough over onto a clean work surface so that the floured side is on the bottom.

To shape the dough into a round loaf (see photos, opposite): Use your fingertips to gently tap and just barely stretch the dough into a loose rectangle, with a short side facing you. Bring the bottom third of the rectangle to the middle, gently tapping along the seam with your fingertips. Stretch the sides of the dough and fold them onto each other so that they overlap, then grasp the short edge farthest from you and fold it over the dough so that it meets the bottom edge.

After you have created this dough envelope, roll the bottom half of the dough onto itself and flip the whole thing over. Slide the bench scraper just underneath the dough at 10 o'clock and make deliberate movements to 3 o'clock, guiding and shaping the dough clockwise into a round with your free hand. The surface of the dough will begin to tighten and become smooth and round, just as it did when pre-shaping the dough. Once you feel there is enough surface tension and you have formed an even and smooth round loaf, set it on the board, seam-side down, for a few minutes. (If making two loaves, repeat for the second loaf.)

To shape the dough into a long loaf (see photos, page 87): Use your fingertips to gently tap the dough into a uniformly round shape. Stretch the dough at 2 o'clock and fold it onto itself toward 8 o'clock. Similarly, stretch the dough at 10 o'clock and fold it onto itself toward 5 o'clock to create a triangle. Take the tip of the triangle that is farthest from you and start rolling it over the dough and toward you. Set your palms on top of the dough and train your thumbs along the front. Roll the dough toward you while pushing it away with your thumbs to create tension on the surface; push the dough away from you without breaking it. Finish shaping the loaf by gently rolling your hands along the length of the dough, beginning in the middle and working your way toward either end.

5. Final Proofing

For the final proof, you will need a medium mixing bowl/basket lined with kitchen towels for each loaf. Dust the proofing basket(s) and the loaf/loaves themselves liberally to prevent the dough from sticking. We use Dusting Flour (page 86), which is a combination of rice flour and all-purpose flour, to coat the proofing baskets/bowls before putting the dough into them. The rice flour prevents the mixture from being absorbed into the dough and also prevents the dough from sticking to the basket. Further, the dusting flour that remains on the proofed dough will protect the crust from caramelizing too fast in the oven.

Slide your bench scraper underneath a loaf and transfer it to the bowl/basket seam-side up. Repeat for the second loaf. Cover the loaves and proof in a draft-free place at room temperature (75°F). Differing proofing times will be specified in each recipe.

DUSTING FLOUR

Whisk together ¼ cup rice flour with ¼ cup all-purpose flour. If you plan to bake often, double or triple the amounts and store the mixture in an airtight container.

6. Score and Bake

To bake the shaped loaf/loaves the same day: If making two loaves, cover one with a kitchen towel and refrigerate up to 1 hour to prevent the dough from further proofing while you score and bake the other one.

To bake the shaped loaf/loaves the next day: Cover the loaf/loaves with a kitchen towel and let proof at room temperature for about 2 hours. This will allow the loaf/loaves to continue proofing until you transfer them to the refrigerator overnight, which will slow down the fermentation process. If the next morning the loaf/loaves look aerated and fully proofed, you can bake right away. If they appear under-proofed, let them sit at room temperature for 1 to 2 hours before baking.

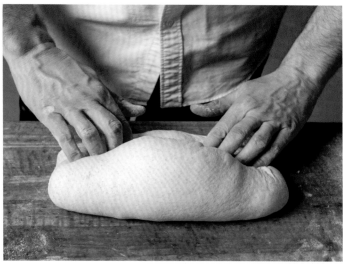 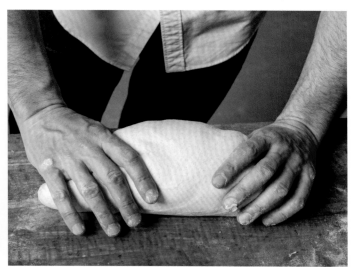

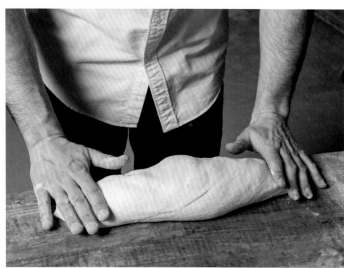 

To bake (see photos): About 45 minutes before the proofing is complete, position a rack in the center of the oven and place a cast-iron combo cooker, Dutch oven, or, for long loaves, a Challenger bread pan (page 339) on it. Preheat the oven to 500°F. Prepare a piece of parchment paper long enough to overhang the sides of the cooker or Dutch oven by 4 inches.

At this point, if you are making two loaves, you will score and bake them one at a time; cover one with a kitchen towel and refrigerate up to 1 hour to prevent it from proofing further while you score and bake the other one.

Wearing sturdy oven mitts, carefully remove the pot from the oven (it will be extremely hot). Remove the lid.

Gently turn the dough out of the basket onto the parchment, seam-side down. Working quickly, use a lame or single-edge razor blade to score the top of the loaf. Hold the corner edge of the blade at a 45-degree angle to the dough and make the cuts between ⅛ inch and ¼ inch deep so that they expand, or bloom, evenly (see photos). For a basic round sourdough loaf, score with 4 slashes to make a large square, with the ends of each score intersecting. Each loaf at the bakery has a particular scoring pattern, with the square being the most basic. You can score the breads in whatever patterns you like; each recipe simply instructs you to score the loaf. Pick up the edges of the parchment and, using it like a sling, set the loaf, parchment and all, into the preheated pot.

SCORE AND BAKE (LONG)

Cover the cooker and slide it onto the oven rack. Bake 20 minutes for a small loaf and 25 minutes for a large loaf, rotating the pot front to back once. Wearing the oven mitts, remove the lid and continue to bake the loaf, uncovered, until the crust is deep, dark brown, 10 to 15 minutes more.

Slide a long-handled offset metal spatula under the loaf as you pry it from the pan and carefully transfer to a cooling rack. Tap the bottom of the loaf; it should sound hollow. If it doesn't, return it to the oven, placing it directly on the oven rack, and bake for 5 minutes more.

7. Cool and Store

Put the loaf/loaves on a rack to allow air to flow around them and let them cool completely (at least 2 hours) before slicing (or tearing apart) and eating—if you can manage to wait that long. Once cooled, an uncut loaf can be covered with a linen towel. Once sliced, store the loaf cut-side down. To store overnight, slide it into an airtight resealable plastic bag. To freeze, cut the bread into slices of even thickness, double wrap in plastic wrap, and freeze up to 2 months.

SCORE AND BAKE (ROUND)

THE
BREADS

LEVAIN BREADS

PANE FRANCESE

MAKES 1 LARGE LOAF

Pane francese literally translates to "French bread." It is one of our naked breads, made up of just water, flour, salt, and time. Ciabatta-like, it originates from northern Italy, where Italy and France meet. Most bread books describe it as a cross between a baguette and a ciabatta. The truth is, I've actually never seen or tasted any other pane francese but the one that made Igor famous when he started his own bakery. When we started our business in New York City, I tried to re-create Igor's version, though to this day I've never asked him what his process was. With a lot of trial and error, we created a bread that is an ode to Igor's creation: the square loaf with three cuts (unlike ciabatta, which is typically rectangular and never scored with a blade). If done right, it should have a beautiful open crumb and big irregular air pockets.

Since pane francese is not pre-shaped or shaped, its strength and structure need to be almost fully developed by the end of the bulk fermentation. There is virtually no shaping apart from minimal stretching to make the sides of the square even, and the proofing happens directly on the floured kitchen towel. While mixing the dough in the bakery, my brother, Hedon, realized, that "Francese loves the 'old' levain, when it's really fully ripened." It wasn't easy to strike a balance between the water percentage, amount of levain, mixing time, bulk fermentation, and folding to create a dough with both enough strength and plenty of elasticity. We had no idea that a high percentage of mature levain in this recipe would reinforce the dough structure. It was just something that he observed that led us to adjust the process. Observe and adjust. Words to live by when you are making bread.

INGREDIENT	BAKER'S PERCENTAGE	WEIGHT (GRAMS)
Water (75°F)	65%	325g
Levain	50%	250g
Bread flour	100%	500g
Salt	2.6%	13g
Bassinage	7%	35g

1. MIX THE DOUGH (step 1, page 78).

2. BULK FERMENT, STRETCH, AND FOLD (step 2, page 81): Bulk fermentation time is 3 hours. Stretch and fold the dough every 45 minutes for the first 2 hours 15 minutes.

RECIPE CONTINUES

3. **SHAPE AND PROOF:** Generously dust the top of the dough, as well as a work surface, with flour. Flip the container over and turn the dough out onto the work surface, taking care not to let it fold on itself. The floured side of the dough should be on the work surface. Stretch the dough slightly to make the opposite edges parallel with each other to form a square. If you want perfect edges, trim them with a dough scraper. Dust the loaf and a large kitchen towel liberally with Dusting Flour (page 86). Place on the kitchen towel and wrap to support the dough so that it holds its square shape. Set aside to proof for 3 hours in a warm (75°F), draft-free spot.

4. **SCORE AND BAKE** (step 6, page 86): Score the loaf and bake for a total of 45 minutes.

5. **COOL AND STORE** (step 7, page 89).

TRADITIONAL SOURDOUGH

MAKES 1 LARGE OR 2 SMALL LOAVES

It took a few years of trial and error after I mixed my first batch of dough in 1993 to come up with a pre-ferment and finally a recipe for a sourdough we were proud to sell. We've been making this one since 1997.

INGREDIENT	BAKER'S PERCENTAGE	WEIGHT (GRAMS)
Water (75°F)	70%	350g
Levain	20%	100g
Bread flour	90%	450g
Dark rye flour	5%	25g
Whole wheat flour	5%	25g
Salt	2.8%	14g
Bassinage	5%	25g

1. MIX THE DOUGH (step 1, page 78).

2. BULK FERMENT, STRETCH, AND FOLD (step 2, page 81): Bulk fermentation time is 3 hours. Stretch and fold the dough every 45 minutes for the first 2 hours 15 minutes.

3. DIVIDE, SHAPE, AND PROOF (steps 3 to 5, pages 82 to 85): Proof for 3 to 5 hours at 75°F or, to bake the next day, proof for 2 hours at 75°F and then refrigerate for 15 to 18 hours.

4. SCORE AND BAKE (step 6, page 86): Score the loaves and bake for a total of 35 to 40 minutes.

5. COOL AND STORE (step 7, page 89).

VARIATION: SEEDED SOURDOUCH
Makes 1 large or 2 small loaves

French Morning, the web magazine and leading online media for French people living in the United States, organizes a bread and pastry competition among the top New York City bakeries every year. We came full circle when in 2019 our seeded sourdough was voted the best specialty bread in the competition. It was especially gratifying since one of the other bakeries participating was Maison Kayser, founded by Éric Kayser, who coauthored the baking books that my mother translated all those years ago.

You can experiment with any seeds you like; either soak them, toast them, or use them raw.

22 grams flaxseeds
22 grams sunflower seeds
22 grams sesame seeds
22 grams poppy seeds
10 grams caraway seeds
20 grams water

1. In a medium bowl, combine half of the seeds and the water and soak for 1 hour. The seeds should soak up all of the water.

2. Follow the steps for Traditional Sourdough (page 101). Do not add the seeds during the mixing process.

3. DIVIDE, SHAPE, AND PROOF (steps 3 to 5, pages 82 to 85): After shaping the loaf/ loaves, spread the remaining dry seeds for coating in an even layer on a half-sheet pan and the remainder divided between the two proofing baskets. As soon as you shape them, roll the loaves all over in the seeds on the sheet pan, to cover completely. Set the loaves, seam-side up in the prepared baskets.

JEWISH-STYLE RYE WITH CARAWAY

MAKES 1 LARGE OR 2 SMALL LOAVES

This was one of the first breads we discovered on arriving in New York, a novelty for us as we had nothing like it at home. Never mind the heaps of pastrami that always seemed to come with it. We couldn't resist but to make our own version of it and say thank you to the city we love.

INGREDIENT	BAKER'S PERCENTAGE	WEIGHT (GRAMS)
Water (75°F)	70%	350g
Levain	40%	200g
Bread flour	90%	450g
Dark rye flour	10%	50g
Salt	3%	15g
Bassinage	5%	25g
Caraway seeds	2.2%	11g

1. **MIX THE DOUGH** (step 1, page 78).

2. **BULK FERMENT, STRETCH, AND FOLD** (step 2, page 81): Bulk fermentation time is 3 hours. Stretch and fold the dough every 45 minutes for the first 2 hours 15 minutes.

3. **DIVIDE, SHAPE, AND PROOF** (steps 3 to 5, pages 82 to 85): Proof for 3 to 5 hours at 75°F or, to bake the following day, proof for 2 hours at 75°F and then refrigerate for 15 to 18 hours.

4. **SCORE AND BAKE** (step 6, page 86): Score the bread and bake for 40 minutes.

5. **COOL AND STORE** (step 7, page 89).

SEVEN-GRAIN

MAKES 1 LARGE OR 2 SMALL LOAVES

We were in our early twenties when we fell in love with what Eli Zabar was doing with his breads. Without any formal bread education or baking experience, we simply gravitated to Eli's without really understanding why. I must admit that we are a little proud of our own taste; without it we would not have had such a beautiful entry into the world of bread. What we tasted, saw, and observed at Eli's inspired us and gave us a rock-solid foundation for years to come.

I have never met Eli Zabar, but I still visit his stores frequently. Over the years I have wondered if Eli had ever said anything to Milan, our friend from Belgrade and Eli's employee, about helping us, the kids who later opened two bakeries inspired by his breads and his work, but I never dared to ask. Milan stayed with Eli long after he helped us and until his passing in 2014.

The bread below is our version of Eli's health bread. Unlike the other sourdoughs, this one is rather dense, with a uniformly tight crumb.

INGREDIENT	BAKER'S PERCENTAGE	WEIGHT (GRAMS)
Water (75°F)	70%	350g
Levain	40%	200g
Wildflower honey	25%	125g
Whole wheat flour	100%	500g
Salt	4%	20g
Active dry yeast	1%	5g (1¼ teaspoons)
Bassinage	5%	25g
Flaxseeds	20%	100g
Sunflower seeds	20%	100g
Sesame seeds	20%	100g
Rolled oats (for coating)		40g

1. **MIX THE DOUGH** (step 1, page 78).

2. **BULK FERMENT, STRETCH, AND FOLD** (step 2, page 81): Bulk fermentation time is 3 hours. Stretch and fold the dough twice every hour for the first 2 hours of the bulk fermentation, or until the dough doesn't pull back.

RECIPE CONTINUES

3. **DIVIDE, SHAPE, AND PROOF** (steps 3 to 5, pages 82 to 85): After shaping the loaf/ loaves, spread half of the rolled oats in an even layer on a half-sheet pan and divide the remainder between the two proofing baskets. Using a spray bottle, spray the loaves lightly with water, then roll them all over in the oats on the sheet pan, to cover completely. Set the loaves seam-side up in the prepared baskets. Proof for 2 to 3 hours at 75°F (there is no need to overnight proof because there is a large proportion of yeast in the dough).

4. **SCORE AND BAKE** (step 6, page 86): Score the bread. For breads containing any kind of a sweetener, in this case honey, we reduce the oven temperature to 450°F immediately after sliding the bread into the oven. Bake for 40 minutes.

5. **COOL AND STORE** (step 7, page 89).

CRANBERRY PECAN SOURDOUGH

MAKES 2 SMALL LOAVES

We couldn't bake this bread fast enough after the *Boston Globe* featured us in fall 1993.

The story was timed to Thanksgiving and came out on the Sunday before the holiday. We were stunned by its immediate result: Customers showed up clutching the article and asking for the exact breads mentioned in the piece, including this one.

This loaf is so loaded with dried cranberries and nuts that the bread is essentially holding them in place. At the bakery, we mix the dough in commercial mixers, which wind up crushing the pecans so small that their flavor is distributed throughout the dough, giving the loaf an overall deeper flavor. To achieve this by hand mixing, crush the nuts before incorporating them: Put them in a resealable plastic bag and pound with a rolling pin or other heavy object. This is a nice bread to serve on a cheese board, the way our restaurant customers do.

INGREDIENT	BAKER'S PERCENTAGE	WEIGHT (GRAMS)
Water (75°F)	70%	350g
Levain	40%	200g
Maple syrup	5.6%	28g
Bread flour	100%	500g
Salt	2.8%	14g
Bassinage	5%	25g
Sun-dried cranberries	34%	170g
Pecan halves, crushed	34%	170g

1. MIX THE DOUGH (step 1, page 78).

2. BULK FERMENT, STRETCH, AND FOLD (step 2, page 81): Bulk fermentation time is 3 hours. Stretch and fold after the first hour, and again after the second hour.

3. DIVIDE, SHAPE, AND PROOF (steps 3 to 5, pages 82 to 85): Shape into 2 long or round loaves. Proof for 3 to 5 hours at 75°F or proof for 2 hours at 75°F and then refrigerate for 15 to 18 hours.

RECIPE CONTINUES

4. **SCORE AND BAKE** (step 6, page 86): Score the loaves. Reduce the oven temperature to 450°F immediately after sliding the bread into the oven. Bake for 35 minutes.

5. **COOL AND STORE** (step 7, page 89).

VARIATIONS

This sourdough bread can handle all manner of substitutions for the cranberries and crushed pecans.

Swap out the cranberries for an equal weight of raisins.

Use 112 grams each (336 grams total) of roughly chopped figs, dried pears, and crushed walnuts.

Use a combination of 112 grams each (336 grams total) of chopped pitted prunes, chopped dried apricots, and crushed pecans. Reduce the bread flour to 225 grams and add 250 grams whole wheat flour and 25 grams dark rye flour.

During the holidays, we make a chocolate hazelnut version with the addition of 170 grams chopped dark chocolate (72% cacao) and 170 grams crushed toasted hazelnuts.

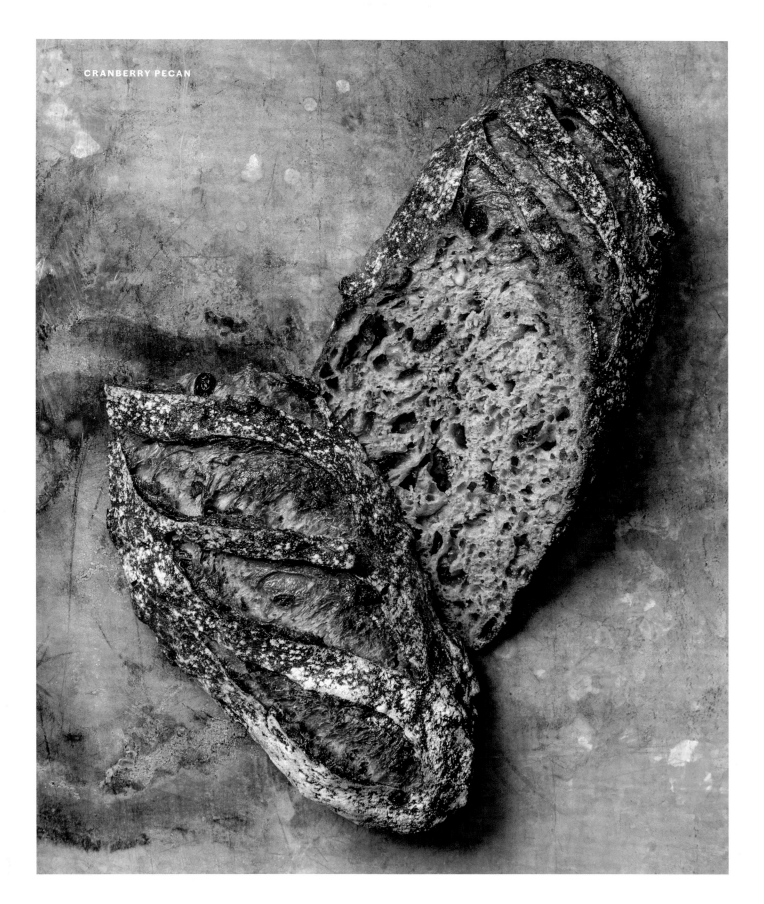

CRANBERRY PECAN

RAISIN PECAN

PRUNE APRICOT PECAN

CHOCOLATE HAZELNUT

KALAMATA OLIVE SOURDOUGH

MAKES 1 LARGE OR 2 SMALL LOAVES

Olives, one of the most recognizable symbols of Mediterranean cuisine, are an essential part of that region's diet and culture. Olive trees, the fruit, and oil are mentioned in every holy book, whether Judaic, Christian, or Islamic. One of the oldest olive trees that still bears fruit every year is located on the island of Brioni in Croatia. It is believed to be 1,600 years old. As with bread, somewhere deep in our emotional memory, olives and olive oil connect to our feeling of comfort and happiness. It was only natural for us to combine the two. In this recipe we use Greek Kalamata olives, which give the crumb a light purple hue, but you can use any olives you like. Don't drain the olives completely; if you add a little bit of brine to the mix, it will only add to the flavor.

INGREDIENT	BAKER'S PERCENTAGE	WEIGHT (GRAMS)
Water (75°F)	70%	350g
Levain	40%	200g
Bread flour	100%	500g
Salt	2.2%	11g
Bassinage	5%	25g
Kalamata olives, quartered	25%	125g

1. **MIX THE DOUGH** (step 1, page 78): After the autolyse, add the olives, brine, salt, and bassinage, and mix with your hands. The dough will be slippery and come apart at first; keep working it until it comes together and the olives are nicely distributed, about 8 minutes.

2. **BULK FERMENT, STRETCH, AND FOLD** (step 2, page 81): Bulk fermentation time is 3 to 4 hours. Stretch and fold the dough every 45 minutes for the first 2 hours 15 minutes.

3. **DIVIDE, SHAPE, AND PROOF** (steps 3 to 5, pages 82 to 85): Proof for 3 to 5 hours at 75°F or proof for 2 hours at 75°F and then refrigerate for 15 to 18 hours.

4. **SCORE AND BAKE** (step 6, page 86): Score the loaf/loaves and bake for 40 minutes.

5. **COOL AND STORE** (step 7, page 89).

ANADAMA

MAKES 1 LARGE ROUND LOAF

Often we receive requests from chefs asking us to do something unique and exclusive for their restaurants. As wholesale bakers, we are not necessarily equipped to take on boutique orders; bread is a living thing, unpredictable and temperamental. Change, we learned the hard way, is the enemy of consistency. So, we typically shied away from special orders. Still, every once in a while, we would meet a chef whose creativity would spark our imagination.

In 2017 the most anticipated restaurant opening in New York City was the makeover of The Grill, the legendary Four Seasons restaurant. After a lot of uncertainty as to who the new operator would be, it was announced that the Major Food Group had won the bid. Bane already had a beautiful relationship with the principals, Mario Carbone, Rich Torrisi, and Jeff Zalaznick, for whom we custom-made a sesame sub-roll used as a sandwich bread for all of their Parm restaurants. We'd been supplying Dirty French as well as other restaurants operated by the group already, and they chose us to help them with their bread program for the opening of The Grill in the Seagram Building.

"Mr. Carbone, Mr. Torrisi, and Mr. Zalaznick prepare for their restaurants the way Matthew Weiner or David Simon get ready for a new show, with a mountain of research," wrote Pete Wells in his three-star review for the *New York Times*. Their *Mad Men*–inspired menu called for bread similar to anadama, a traditional New England bread made with wheat, cornmeal, and molasses. A few years earlier, Chad Robertson had published his third baking book, in which he introduced a new method of incorporating grains with no gluten to his breads by cooking the grains first into a porridge and adding them later to the already developed dough, the same way seeds and nuts are incorporated. This way, he managed to preserve the crumb and crust texture of the traditionally made sourdough, while adding more flavor and more hydration to the dough. The result is a significantly extended shelf life and a variety of new flavors. This inspired us to deconstruct anadama bread completely while using the original ingredients to rebuild it. You can use any grain you wish—barley, millet, emmer, rice, corn, oats, quinoa—and make a porridge that you will later add to the dough. The amount of porridge you can incorporate into a dough can vary from 30% to 50% of the total flour weight. For the anadama, we use 30% of the total flour weight.

RECIPE CONTINUES

INGREDIENT	BAKER'S PERCENTACE	WEIGHT (CRAMS)
Water (80°F)	75%	375g
Levain	15%	75g
Molasses	5%	25g
Bread flour	40%	200g
Whole wheat flour	60%	300g
Bassinage	10%	50g
Salt	2.6%	13g
Polenta (recipe follows)	30%	150g

1. **MIX THE DOUCH** (step 1, page 78). Do not add the polenta during the mixing process.

2. **BULK FERMENT, STRETCH, AND FOLD** (step 2, page 81): Bulk fermentation time is 3½ hours. Stretch and fold the dough 4 times every 45 minutes, scattering one-quarter of the polenta over the dough before each fold.

3. **SHAPE AND PROOF** (steps 3 to 5, pages 82 to 85): Proof for 3 to 5 hours at 75°F or proof for 2 hours at 75°F and then refrigerate for 15 to 18 hours.

4. **SCORE AND BAKE** (step 6, page 86): Score the loaf and bake for 50 minutes.

5. **COOL AND STORE** (step 7, page 89).

POLENTA

For the polenta, we use a 2:1 ratio of water to cornmeal with a pinch of salt.

Makes enough for 1 large loaf

50 grams cornmeal
100 grams water
Pinch of salt

In a saucepan, combine the cornmeal, water, and salt and bring to a boil. Reduce the heat to low and simmer, whisking often, until the polenta starts to thicken, about 5 minutes. The polenta mixture should still be slightly loose. Cover and cook for 30 minutes, whisking every 5 to 6 minutes. When the polenta gets too thick to whisk, stir with a wooden spoon. Remove and spread on a flat surface and let cool before using.

Beyond the Swinging Door: an Immigrant's View—from the Outside Looking In

Among my first jobs at the bakery on Cape Cod was driving the delivery car to Boston. I liked those early-morning drives to Boston. I liked Boston itself. It reminded me of home—small and split into two distinct places. The Charles River is to Boston and Cambridge what the Danube is to Belgrade and New Belgrade.

One of the restaurants we delivered to was called The Top of the Hub. It was perched on the city's tallest building, which we nicknamed the CK, an abbreviation for the building in Belgrade that was home to the Central Kommittee of the Communist Party.

In those early days, delivering bread to the big hotels—The Four Seasons, The Westin, The Marriott—was quite scary. The loading docks and the world hidden just beyond them rattled me. Those massive mouths—the receiving guts of the city, where five tractor-trailer trucks could pull in at once and unload—seemed unnoticed by pedestrians rushing by. The magnitude of these spaces, where there is little sign of life apart from a security guard ensconced in his booth, muttering a word or two, felt cold and unsettling.

In every restaurant kitchen, however, the scene looked familiar. Each was filled with the same mix of people working at the bakery—and they looked similar to the employees in every other food venue that took our deliveries. These were the people behind the scenes, making it all happen. And most of them were immigrants. They work in kitchens that are, metaphorically speaking, miles away from the dining room. Those loading docks and hives of activity barely registered to the hundreds of thousands of people who walked through the establishments' *front* doors. In the "back of the house," a team of immigrants working just to survive were preparing $50 bowls of soup.

Often, Vojin or Bane had sales calls with chefs during their downtime, which meant the tastings took place in empty dining rooms. The progression from the foreboding docks to the kitchen to the dining room is itself a metaphor for the great American dream, but it is the swinging door separating the kitchen from the dining room that I found most symbolic. It divides two very different worlds: on one side immigrants are working to pay for their next meal, while on the other sit some of the wealthiest people in town. It is an image that has stayed with me to this day.

Why do people migrate? What would possess anyone to voluntarily leave an entire life behind? A better life. Better opportunities. Access to freedoms that have been stripped from them. People will always migrate; nothing will stop them. There is a misconception that immigrants and refugees bring harm to nations, but the truth is they contribute to growth, innovation, economic stimulation, and expansion.

It's impossible to imagine what it means to be an immigrant if you have never been one. Everything you once knew ceases to exist. For us, the war, the destruction, the breakup of our country, were obviously terrible. To leave it all behind and start all over, however, was unthinkable. Of course, we were the lucky ones; unlike so many others, we had support from our parents, enough to get us on a plane and out of our homeland.

Yet, that was only the beginning. It took some time after arriving in the US to feel visible. For me, this was magnified exponentially because by nature, actors crave attention. This came into stark relief when I found myself in the emergency room after a heavy piece of oven equipment landed on my foot during a move at the bakery. There were stacks of papers to fill out, but I only had my name and address to write down. My dream then was that I would one day have what was required—a social security card and medical insurance documents—to properly fill out those forms.

Though we didn't have everything we needed in those early days, we were lucky to have each other. We learned that the greatest resource we had in building our business was our strong bond to one another. Not only did it inform our business philosophy, but it influenced how we came to grow our team of mostly immigrant employees. When I look around the bakery today, I am reminded of those first years away from the comfort and familiarity of home, when we were driven by a burning desire to connect in an unfamiliar place. All of us, then and now, are drawn to the promise of building on human relationships like those formed every day in restaurant kitchens, a stone's throw from the dining room, but in so many ways, worlds away.

David Palta,
Production

I came to the States in 1990 from Cuenca in southern Ecuador because the economy was bad. My father was already here. He and two friends came through Tijuana in the 1970s, eventually making it to Jackson Heights, Queens, where they became dishwashers.

I paid a coyote to make the escape plan that would get me to the States. He charged me $7,000, which I collected from friends and neighbors. I used my father's house as a guarantee. With two friends, I flew from Quito to Guatemala, then took a taxi to the border of Mexico. We waded across the Usumacinta River in water that went up to our chins, and once in Mexico, took an hour-long taxi ride to meet the bus that would take us to Mexico City. The bus was packed with migrants; the coyote gave us a bottle of water and put the three of us inside the casing that holds the motor. It was so tight that you couldn't lift your arm to drink the water. And the fumes were terrible.

It felt like my life was over once that box was closed. We were inside it for three days, hot during the day and very cold at night. No one checked on us. It was so hard not to feel like this was the end. The only thing that kept

me alive was thinking about my family. I stayed alive for them.

We were supposed to go to Tijuana from Mexico City, but instead we were dropped off somewhere outside the city. Our coyote disappeared, which is common. We had no idea where we were. There were others trying to cross the border, but the police were everywhere. We hid in the bushes and then got lost. For two weeks, we walked, ate nothing, and drank from the river.

Lucky for us, a family helped us by giving us food and paying for a cab back to Mexico City. We got a new coyote, who charged us $5,000 for the remainder of the journey. He gave us spicy chicken soup, the most delicious food I ever ate.

The new coyote got us fake documents and partnered us with women who pretended to be our wives (being married makes it easier to pass through). We flew from Mexico City to Tijuana, scared to death.

We sat at the border for two days waiting for the police to change shifts. As soon as they leave their post, you run. The first time we got halfway across before they started chasing us, so we ran back. It took us two more tries. Helicopters circled overhead. On the other side, we hid under cars when they shone their lights on us. We walked for another hour, then got in a van that took us to a room in a warehouse with four hundred other migrants. We waited three days for the payment from my family to go through. We then flew out of San Diego and landed at LaGuardia Airport in New York City with nothing but the clothes on our backs. No identification, no papers, nothing.

As we descended into LaGuardia, I saw the New York City of my dreams—the lights, the beauty. On the ground, however, reality set in quickly. My first job was in food delivery by bicycle, yet I had no idea how to ride one. So, in the beginning I just pushed the bike and walked with the food. My next restaurant job offered more opportunity. By the time I left it, I was taking orders in the front of the house. I drove a taxi at night with no license.

The whole time, my dad was working to get my papers.

When I arrived at Pain d'Avignon almost twenty years ago, I drove the delivery van. Now, I am also baking and overseeing the bread production. I love baking the most, being at the oven.

We are all treated like family here, like equals—there is no distinction between bosses and employees. A few years ago, my car broke down and I began walking to work. Bane, Uliks, and Tole noticed and bought me a minivan to get to work and also to use for deliveries. There are so many opportunities here at the bakery; you just have to take advantage. What I appreciate more than anything is that I feel happy here. I would make that trip all over again, knowing what I know now.

POOLISH BREADS and a CLASSIC BAGUETTE

Poolish, or sponge, as we call it in the bakery, is more of a batter than a true dough—a loose, high-hydration combination of equal parts flour and water, with a touch of yeast to push the fermentation along. By its name we can assume its Polish origins, and by its bakery name we can assume its soft and bubbly attributes. Unlike levain, which is refreshed every day, poolish is made from scratch and can be used only once. In the early days, this was the pre-ferment we preferred, likely because the flavor and aroma of the breads made with poolish resembled the breads that we grew up eating: moist, chewy, and with a subtly sweet, fermented flavor, though not sour. You can adjust the amount of yeast in the starter in order to speed or slow the fermentation, but the results will be different. Poolish can be ready to mix into a dough in as little as 3 hours or as soon as it passes a Float Test (page 68), yet we ferment ours for 15 hours; every night we make fresh poolish for the next day. It's up to you to decide how long you wish to ferment yours in search of that perfect crumb structure and more nuanced flavor.

POOLISH

Make the poolish 15 hours before you plan to mix your dough.

INGREDIENT	BAKER'S PERCENTAGE	WEIGHT (GRAMS)
Active dry yeast	0.40%	1g (pinch)
Water (75°F)	100%	250g
Bread flour	100%	250g

1. Put the yeast in a 2-quart transparent container (we use a Cambro storage container, but a glass bowl works really well, too) and pour the water over it. Swirl the yeast and water mixture until it dissolves. Add the flour and mix using a rubber spatula. Scrape the sides of the container with the spatula, turning the bowl as you go and mixing until there are no dry particles remaining. (Pay close attention to the bottom of the bowl, because this is where those particles hide.)

2. Cover and leave at warm room temperature (75°F) for 2 hours, then transfer to the refrigerator overnight. The next day you will notice that the poolish has at least doubled in size, the surface should be bubbly and appear somewhat active, and it should smell faintly sweet (the opposite of sourdough starter). And it should also pass the Float Test (page 68).

COUNTRY BREAD

MAKES 1 LARGE LOAF

This was our favorite bread for a long time. It is what helped us start our deeply cherished relationship with Whole Foods over twenty years ago. At the time, I was reading about communal bakeries of the past and families who had the opportunity to make bread only once a week. Therefore, the bread they baked had to be large enough to last for a week and it had to be fermented in such a way that it would stay fresh until the following week. We made these huge 5- and 10-pound round breads that in my mind resembled the breads of those communal bakeries. There is a lot of poolish in this bread, and it impacts the characteristics of the final dough in a major way. The poolish ferments at room temperature for 2 to 3 hours and is then transferred to the refrigerator to continue fermenting overnight. It will be fully fermented in the morning and will be a bubbly, creamy batter without turning acidic. The idea is to make a bread with the same attributes as those made with a natural starter but without the sour aftertaste.

INGREDIENT	BAKER'S PERCENTAGE	WEIGHT (GRAMS)
Water (75°F)	55%	275g
Poolish (page 135)	100%	500g
Bread flour	90%	450g
Dark rye flour	5%	25g
Whole wheat flour	5%	25g
Salt	3%	15g

1. **MIX THE DOUGH** (step 1, page 78).

2. **BULK FERMENT, STRETCH, AND FOLD** (step 2, page 81): Bulk fermentation time is 4 hours. Stretch and fold after 1 hour; repeat 1 hour later.

3. **SHAPE AND PROOF** (steps 3 to 5, pages 82 to 85): Proof for 1 hour at 75°F, then cold proof in the refrigerator for 5 hours.

4. **SCORE AND BAKE** (step 6, page 86): Score the loaf and bake for 45 minutes.

5. **COOL AND STORE** (step 7, page 89).

CIABATTA

MAKES 2 LOAVES

Good ciabatta can have the same attributes of greatness as pasta or pizza. Simple, yet irresistible. This recipe is inspired by the poor baker trying to make ends meet by adding more water to his dough and skipping the shaping step, in order to lower his costs and increase his margins. But while just trying to get by, he creates something incredible along the way. Not a single loaf of this unshaped high-hydration bread will look the same. Its comforting character and appearance connects us to the times when the beauty of the craft was appreciated and respected. This dough really gives your hands a workout; don't be afraid to work it thoroughly. As we like to say in the bakery, YOU ARE THE BOSS OF THE DOUGH. Like the Pane Francese (95), ciabatta does not need shaping. As another option, I also like to make this bread at home in a Challenger bread pan (page 339).

INGREDIENT	BAKER'S PERCENTAGE	WEIGHT (GRAMS)
Water (75°F)	60%	300g
Poolish (page 135)	80%	400g
Bread flour	100%	500g
Salt	2.6%	13g
Active dry yeast	0.13%	0.66g (¼ teaspoon)
Bassinage	10%	50g

1. **MIX THE DOUGH** (step 1, page 78).

2. **BULK FERMENT, STRETCH, AND FOLD** (step 2, page 81): Bulk fermentation time is 3 hours. Stretch and fold after 45 minutes; repeat for a total of 3 folds.

3. **DIVIDE:** You do not need to shape the dough. Using the dough scraper, divide the dough in half lengthwise into two rectangular pieces. Gently coax each piece of dough into a 12 × 4-inch rectangle, squaring off the sides so that the opposing sides are parallel to each other.

RECIPE CONTINUES

4. **PROOF** (step 5, page 85): Transfer the loaves directly to a flour-dusted working board. Proof for 20 minutes, or until the dough has relaxed. Meanwhile, position an oven rack in the center of the oven and place a baking stone on the rack. Alternatively, place a bread pan on the rack. Preheat the oven to 500°F. Once the oven reaches the desired temperature, dust the loaves with a little flour and flip over onto parchment paper. Slide the loaves, paper and all, onto the baking stone (or, using the parchment like a sling, into the bread pan).

5. **BAKE:** This bread does not need scoring. Throw one ice cube into each corner of the oven (only if using the baking stone) and close the door. Bake for 30 minutes (if you are using a bread pan, remove the top midway through baking).

6. **COOL AND STORE** (step 7, page 89).

VARIATION: MINI CIABATTAS
At the dividing step, cut the dough into 75-gram pieces (you should get about 10) and proceed to proof and bake as directed. You will have to bake them in two or three batches—refrigerate the unbaked dough in the meantime. Bake for 15 minutes, then rotate the stone. Bake until golden and hollow when tapped on the bottom, about 5 minutes more. Let cool on a rack.

"FOCAZZA"

MAKES TWO 13 × 18-INCH FLATBREADS

Not exactly focaccia, not quite pizza, this is ciabatta dough hand pressed into half-sheet pans (we also make them round at the café) and indented all over with your fingertips to catch the pools of olive oil you drizzle on top.

Dough for Ciabatta (page 139)

All-purpose flour, for dusting

Olive oil, for drizzling

Flaky salt, such as Maldon, for sprinkling

1. Make the ciabatta dough as directed through the second folding and resting.

2. DIVIDE, PRE-SHAPE, AND PROOF: Generously flour a work surface as well as a large cutting board. Using a dough scraper, loosen the dough from the container (if necessary, sprinkle flour lightly into the crevices around the edges to help loosen it). Turn the dough out onto the work surface, being careful not to let it fold onto itself (it will spread a bit). Using the dough scraper, divide the dough in half. Each piece should weigh roughly 625 grams.

Shape the dough into balls. Slide the scraper under the dough at the 10 o'clock position and with a sweeping motion, swing it to 3 o'clock, guiding the dough with your other hand to shape it into a loose ball. Transfer onto the board and tap flour through a sieve over each to lightly dust. Place an overturned plastic bin over the dough and set aside to proof in a warm (75°F), draft-free spot until it passes the Fingertip Test (page 76) and is about double in size, 1½ to 2 hours. About 30 minutes before the proofing is completed, position two racks in the center of the oven and preheat to 500°F.

3. SHAPE AND BAKE: Lightly coat two half-sheet pans (13 × 18-inch) with olive oil and place a ball of dough in the middle of each. Using your fingertips, push the dough out to the edges, turning the pan 90 degrees after each push. If the dough resists stretching, cover with the plastic bin and let rest for 10 minutes or so. Once the dough comfortably reaches the edges of the pan, use your fingertips to make indentations all over it; if they do not remain indented, cover the dough with the bin and let rest a bit longer. Once the indentations remain, liberally drizzle olive oil over the dough, then sprinkle salt evenly but sparingly all over.

Bake until the focazzas are deep golden brown, 20 to 25 minutes, switching racks and rotating the pans front to back once. Transfer to a rack to cool.

VARIATION

After drizzling with olive oil in step 3, top the dough with chopped fresh rosemary and pitted, sliced Kalamata or other favorite olives, and cherry tomatoes, then drizzle more olive oil over and bake.

WHITE FRENCH PULLMAN

MAKES 1 LARGE LOAF

Baked in a long, narrow, straight-sided pan, this bread got its name from its use in the kitchens of Pullman railway cars. And the truth is, it actually resembles a train car. In French it is known as *pain de mie*; whatever you call it, it is what packaged sandwich bread wants to be. Of all of our breads, the Pullman has the finest crumb and most delicate texture. Unlike many Pullman recipes, we do not enrich the dough with milk or sugar.

INGREDIENT	BAKER'S PERCENTAGE	WEIGHT (GRAMS)
Water (75°F)	55%	275g
Poolish (page 135)	55%	275g
Bread flour	100%	500g
Salt	3%	15g
Active dry yeast	0.2%	1g (⅓ teaspoon)
Rice bran oil, for the pan		

1. MIX THE DOUGH (step 1, page 78).

2. BULK FERMENT, STRETCH, AND FOLD (step 2, page 81): Bulk fermentation time is 4 hours. There is no stretching and folding. After 2 hours, however, punch down the dough to de-gas and do so again after the third hour.

3. SHAPE AND PROOF (steps 3 to 5, pages 82 to 85): Lightly coat a 13 × 4 × 4-inch Pullman pan with rice bran oil. Shape the dough into a long loaf. Tuck the ends under, stretch it a bit, and gently lay it seam-side down in the loaf pan. Proof for 3 to 5 hours at 75°F or proof for 2 hours at 75°F and then refrigerate for 15 to 18 hours.

4. SCORE AND BAKE (step 6, page 86): Preheat the oven to 500°F. Working quickly, use a lame or single-edge razor blade to score the top of the loaf. Throw one ice cube into each of the corners of the oven and close the door. Bake for 40 minutes.

5. COOL AND STORE (step 7, page 89).

CLASSIC BAGUETTE

MAKES 3 BAGUETTES

In 2006, we received a phone call from the food reporters at *New York* magazine, asking us to send one of our baguettes over immediately. They didn't say why, and we didn't ask. We just picked one up off the shelf and sent it off on the regular delivery truck. A few weeks later, without any warning, the magazine published a bread article titled "Monsieur Baguette" featuring Steve Kaplan, a professor of European history at Cornell University, and widely known as one of the biggest ambassadors of French bread in the world. Kaplan is the author of *Cherchez le pain*, a Zagat-like publication that rates Parisian bread by its appearance, crust, crumb, aroma, and flavor. This was the first time he'd agreed to talk about US bakeries since, in his opinion, there hadn't been much to talk about up until then. He tested baguettes from the top thirteen bakeries in New York City, including ours. All the big guys participated: Balthazar, Eli's, Amy's, Sullivan Street, and Le Pain Quotidien. He rated our baguette second only to the one from Almondine, a small retail bakery in DUMBO, Brooklyn, owned by Jacques Torres, the famed pastry chef turned chocolatier. So, in fact, among wholesale bakeries, ours was rated the best. Mr. Kaplan liked the tactility of its crust, the articulation of its crumb, and its elegance, which he compared to a Dior or Balenciaga runway model. The only thing he did not appreciate were the crackly blisters formed on the crust as a result of a long cold fermentation. It was a huge endorsement for us—but more important, it pushed us to further understand our craft.

When we moved to New York City, we changed the way we made baguettes. Up until then, we had made the dough with a high percentage of poolish, which wasn't holding up too well in the refrigerator during the lengthy cold final proofing. Since we loved the transformation of the crust caused by a long retarding process, we wanted to make a baguette capable of handling this while preserving the lightness of the poolish baguette. We opted for a method that uses a small quantity of previously made dough, one that was not overly fermented. This allowed us to retard the baguettes overnight without over-proofing them or making them acidic. The prolonged fermentation added depth to the flavor, the crust became crispier, and the loaf was able to take on more color while baking without burning. After Mr. Kaplan's review, we reduced the retarding time in half and came closer to making the baguette of our dreams.

Making baguettes at home has its distinct pleasures—and a few challenges. At the bakery, we use dough with a slightly higher hydration percentage than in the recipe below. That is intentional; you will have an easier time handling a dough that is not so loose. One of the critical aspects of turning out a baguette with a decent crust is steam. Our deck ovens feature injectors that produce billows of steam to fill the oven cavity. Since the Dutch

RECIPE CONTINUES

oven isn't suited for these long breads, the steam must be created in a different way. The baguettes are baked directly on the baking stone, and as soon as they are loaded into the oven, ice cubes tossed onto the hot oven floor create the steam needed for the proper oven spring and crust caramelization.

PÂTE FERMENTÉE

Fermented dough, or *pâte fermentée*, is the third type of pre-ferment we use in the bakery to make baguettes and brioche. In an ideal scenario, you make baguettes or brioche one day and use the leftover dough to make more the next day. The dough should not be overly fermented, 3 to 4 hours of bulk fermentation at room temperature or up to 18 hours, and even longer, if refrigerated. Of course, this method is not entirely realistic for the home baker, but you might consider it if time allows for one more day of bread baking. You can use any other dough made with poolish, like White French Pullman (page 144), Ciabatta (page 139), or Country Bread (page 136). If you have none, you can use a very young levain instead.

INGREDIENT	BAKER'S PERCENTAGE	WEIGHT (GRAMS)
Water (75°F)	65%	325g
Pâte fermentée (young levain)	30%	150g
Bread flour	100%	500g
Salt	2.8%	14g
Active dry yeast	0.03%	0.15g
Bassinage	5%	25g

1. MIX THE DOUGH (step 1, page 78).

2. FOLD (step 2, page 81): Bulk fermentation time is 2 hours. Stretch and fold the dough once after 1 hour.

3. DIVIDE: Set a cutting board big enough to hold three loaves nearby. With a dough scraper, loosen the dough from the container. Flip the container over onto the work surface, being careful not to let the dough fold onto itself. (If it does fold onto itself, use the dough scraper to coax it apart.) Cut and weigh the dough into three 275-gram pieces. You will make three baguettes, and the remaining dough will be used tomorrow as your pâte fermentée starter. Put the piece of starter dough in a container with a tight-fitting lid and refrigerate.

RECIPE CONTINUES

4. **PRE-SHAPE** (step 3, page 82): Place the dough, seam-side down, on the resting board, cover with a kitchen towel, and set aside to rest in a warm (75°F), draft-free spot for 20 minutes.

5. **SHAPE:** Place a large linen towel or couche on a large cutting board or overturned half-sheet pan and coat liberally with Dusting Flour (page 86).

Touch each piece of dough with your palm. If sticky, dust a handful of flour onto a clean work surface. If smooth and not at all tacky, skip the flour.

With a dough scraper, flip each loaf from the board onto the work surface. With a long side facing you and with a gentle touch, partially press down the dough to even thickness with your palms—take care not to deflate it too much. Lift the dough to prevent it from sticking to the work surface and gently stretch it before you put it back on the work surface. Working with one piece at a time, fold the top two-thirds of the dough onto itself, sealing the seam gently with your fingertips. Rotate the piece 180 degrees and repeat. Then fold the dough over itself lengthwise while pushing with your thumb inward along the seam while

sealing it with the palm of your other hand. The dough should look like a stubby baguette. Using the palms of your hands, and with your thumbs set against the seam, roll the dough into a uniformly thick 12-inch-long tube, sealing the seams with your thumbs as you roll. Working from the center outward, use your palms to roll the tube out to a 15-inch-long baguette; you may need to do this once or twice. Taper the ends by applying pressure to the "tails" as you roll the dough away from you. Repeat with the remaining dough.

6. **PROOF:** Using the dough scraper, loosen the loaves from the work surface and gently transfer them to the towel or couche, seam-side up, spacing them 2 inches apart. Make a pleat in the towel on either side of the loaves to create "walls" that will help the loaves retain their shape. Give each baguette a liberal dusting of flour by tapping the flour onto them through a sieve. Cover with a kitchen towel and set aside to proof in a warm (75°F), draft-free spot until the loaves have grown in height and expanded in volume, about 45 minutes. If any part of the seam is split, pinch it together with your fingers. Put the baguettes in the refrigerator for at least 1 hour or up to 12 hours.

RECIPE CONTINUES

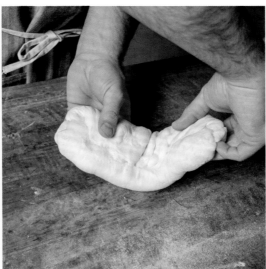

7. SCORE AND BAKE: About 30 minutes before you are ready to bake, prepare a sheet of parchment paper the same size as your baking stone and place it on the back of a sheet pan or on a baking peel. Position a rack in the center of the oven and place the stone on it. Preheat the oven to 500°F.

Gently transfer the baguettes from the couche to the parchment by sliding a flipping board (see page 339) underneath each, and rolling them over onto the parchment so that they are seam-side down. Score the loaves with three vertical cuts on an angle spanning the length of the dough.

Wearing long, sturdy oven mitts and using the parchment like a sling, gently transfer the baguettes onto the stone (pull the oven rack out)—parchment and all. Throw one ice cube into each corner of the oven and close the door. Bake until golden all over, about 15 minutes, then open the door to let the steam out and bake until the crust is deep, dark golden and the ends of the baguettes curve upward, 5 to 8 minutes more. Transfer to a wire rack to cool.

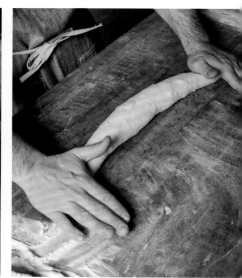

VARIATION: OLIVE BAGUETTE WITH A TOUCH OF ROSEMARY

Combine ¾ cup pitted and quartered green olives of your choice with 1 tablespoon chopped rosemary and add when you Mix the Dough (step 1, page 78).

VARIATION: THYME BAGUETTE WITH A TOUCH OF LEMON

Daniel Humm became an executive chef at the restaurant Eleven Madison Park in Manhattan in early 2006. At that time, we'd been supplying the restaurant with breads. Almost a year into Mr. Humm's tenure, his cooking was going to be reviewed by the *New York Times*, so he wanted to change his bread offerings in order to stand out. He asked us if we could make a bread with chestnut flour that would capture the flavor and spirit of fall and winter and the holiday season. After a few attempts, it was clear to all of us that this wouldn't work since we had no experience with incorporating large quantities of flour with no gluten into the bread. Chef Humm then suggested we make him a dinner roll with lemon zest and fresh thyme. For the next three months we would pick up the fresh thyme from their restaurant and bake the specialty rolls for Eleven Madison Park, which then went on to receive a three-star review from Pete Wells. Here is the baguette version of those rolls.

Add 10 grams finely chopped thyme and the grated zest of 1 lemon when you Mix the Dough (step 1, page 78).

THYME BAGUETTE
WITH A TOUCH
OF LEMON

OLIVE BAGUETTE
WITH A TOUCH
OF ROSEMARY

Cleberson Lemos,

Head of Production, Cape Cod

I was eighteen years old and living in the small city of Conselheiro Pena in Brazil when I decided to come to the US. My brother was living here, so the path was somewhat paved for me. But not entirely. I spoke no English at all, getting a visa was not easy, and I would be traveling alone and for the first time. Plus, my dad made me promise that I would return home after two years. It was hard to look him in the eye, because I knew that I would probably stay in the US forever.

Getting a visa meant a ten-hour bus ride to Rio de Janeiro. But worse than that, my young age meant that my father had to sign a document that made me an emancipated minor in order to travel alone. Symbolically, this must have been very difficult for him.

I was lucky to arrive in the States to a brother who had an established business, a restaurant in Hyannis,

Massachusetts. He connected me with the owners of Pain d'Avignon and I started working right away. In the beginning, I had to use my hands to communicate. All the while, I was paying very close attention to how the bread was baked, so that one day I might be able to take on that job. I went from sweeping floors to mixing, cutting, shaping, and baking the dough. Eventually I became the production manager. This was so challenging because my English was still pretty weak. I had so much responsibility and much of it interacting with people—placing orders, training employees, managing schedules among them.

For all of the challenges—learning a new language, a new culture, a new kind of work—I have only gratitude. I made one of the best decisions of my life when I decided to come to the United States. Not only do I have the privilege of work that I truly love, but I met my wife here, and together we have three beautiful children. For the last twenty-five years, my life has been so full and it continues to be exciting every day. It does not get any better than that.

BRIOCHE

Brioche lives in a unique category. Not quite bread, not quite pastry, it belongs to both yet stands on its own. In fact, it can be whatever you want it to be. You can treat it like a bread: slice it, toast it, and if you make a bun, slide a burger into it. Or it can be a beautiful pastry, filled with chocolate or candied fruits. It can be laminated the same way croissants are.

Brioche is a pretty complex dough to make, but once you succeed, you will find the results are entirely worth it. Like most European breads that contain eggs, milk, and a fair amount of butter, brioche belongs to the family of breads born during festive holidays and end-of-year religious celebrations, when, in otherwise leaner times, families allow themselves to add these precious, expensive ingredients to their basic breads. The butter acts as a tenderizer for the dough—it coats and shortens the gluten strands—and makes the crust soft and the crumb tender.

Brioche dough is a little colder than other bread doughs, since the milk and eggs used to hydrate the flour come directly from the refrigerator. Another note: The brioche should bulk ferment both at room temperature and in the refrigerator.

BUTTER: THE MAGIC INGREDIENT

Butter is a primary ingredient in brioche; only eggs claim a greater baker's percentage. It is the addition of such a substantial amount of butter that makes preparing the dough a bit challenging to master. But there's magic in that butter. It may seem like you are adding heft to the dough as you mix it in, but the end result is bread that is soft, silky, and light as a feather. The key to successfully incorporating the butter into the dough lies in its consistency. It must be firm but pliable. The best way to achieve this is to take the butter straight from the fridge and beat it flat with a rolling pin while it is still wrapped in paper. When it softens to the point you can make a hole in it with your finger with minimal effort, it is the right consistency. Alternatively, you can remove the butter from the refrigerator about 1 hour (depending on the room temperature) before you plan to mix the dough; it should be supple yet still cold. At the bakery, of course, we use a heavy-duty mixer to incorporate the butter into the dough, but in the spirit of developing a feel for it, I want you to mix it by hand. It's a workout—if you are not up for it, then by all means use a stand mixer fitted with the dough hook.

Once you begin, it will appear as if the butter is stubbornly remaining apart from the dough, that it will never become a cohesive mass. Persevere!

BASIC BRIOCHE DOUGH

MAKES ENOUGH FOR 2 SMALL PULLMAN LOAVES, 12 BUNS, 24 SLIDERS, OR 12 STICKY BUNS

INGREDIENT	BAKER'S PERCENTAGE	WEIGHT (GRAMS)
Bread flour	100%	500g
Milk	10%	50g
Eggs	50%	250g
Sugar	14%	70g
Pâte fermentée (or young levain)	20%	100g
Salt	2%	10g
Active dry yeast	1.4%	7g (2½ teaspoons)
Unsalted butter, cut into ½-inch cubes, at room temperature (about 65°F)	40%	200g
Rice bran or other neutral-flavored oil, for the container		

1. **MIX THE DOUGH:** In a large mixing bowl, combine the flour, milk, eggs, and sugar and add fistfuls of the pâte fermentée to it. Use a rubber spatula to loosely combine the ingredients, then continue using a wet hand. Mix the dough, rotating the bowl as you work your way around it to incorporate the ingredients, then fold it onto itself. Scrape down the sides if the dough is sticking to the bowl. You will work the dough this way until it is dense and stiff but smooth, about 15 minutes.

Sprinkle the salt and yeast in discrete piles over the dough. Cover with a kitchen towel and set aside to proof in a room-temperature (75°F), draft-free spot for 30 minutes.

Begin to incorporate the butter in two additions. Squeeze half of the butter pieces through your hands and onto the dough. Fold the dough onto itself and press firmly on it, incorporating the butter into the fold. The butter pieces may fall away from the dough; scoop them with a cupped hand and incorporate them into the dough as you rotate the bowl with your other hand. Next, fold and press down on the dough with your palm, still rotating the bowl and continuing to fold the dough onto itself as you press firmly on it. The dough will begin to incorporate the butter completely. Add the remaining half of the butter pieces and incorporate as before, rotating the bowl as you work your way around it. The butter may fall away as you work it in; keep squeezing, folding, and pushing on the dough. Your hands will get a workout! As the butter becomes completely incorporated, the dough will begin to feel springier, becoming smoother and shinier, if slightly tacky. Expect to knead the dough in the bowl this way for 15 to 20 minutes.

2. BULK FERMENT: Cover the mixing bowl with a kitchen towel and let it proof in a warm room-temperature (75°F), draft-free spot until it has relaxed and spreads a bit, and it passes the Windowpane Test (page 81), about 1 hour.

Coat a 4-quart storage container with rice bran oil. Fold the dough (page 81) and transfer it to the oiled container, cover with plastic wrap, and refrigerate for 4 to 6 hours.

After 2 hours, fold and de-gas the dough to strengthen it and to even out the temperature. The dough should be stiff and cold all the way through, which will allow you to shape it easily.

3. SHAPE AND BAKE: Using a dough scraper, loosen the dough from the edge of the container and turn it out onto a clean work surface. (If the dough sticks to the work surface, dust the work surface very lightly with flour.) Follow the individual recipe instructions to shape and bake the brioche.

BRIOCHE LOAVES

MAKES 2 SMALL LOAVES

This recipe makes two 9 × 4 × 4-inch loaves; if you want to make a single large loaf, use a 13 × 4 × 4-inch Pullman pan.

Basic Brioche Dough (page 164)   1 large egg, for egg wash

1. **MIX AND BULK FERMENT** the brioche dough as directed.

2. **DIVIDE AND SHAPE:** Line two 9 × 4 × 4-inch Pullman pans with parchment paper to hang over the long sides.

Using the dough scraper, divide the dough evenly into two pieces.

Working with one piece of dough at a time, flatten it with your fingertips to form a 9-inch oval with a long "side" facing you. Fold the top third of the dough toward you and onto itself (the edge will land two-thirds of the way down the dough), pressing gently along the seam. Grasp the two top "corners" of the dough that were created from the previous fold, and bring them to the center of the seam and press gently with your fingertips. Roll the dough toward you again, two-thirds of the way down the dough, then press firmly along the seam with your fingertips. Roll again to the edge of the dough and press firmly along the seam. The dough will begin to look like a cylinder. Using your palms, roll the loaf back and forth a few times to elongate it by an inch or two, until it is about 6 inches long, keeping the seam on the bottom. Tuck the sides under and place the loaf in the prepared pan. Repeat with the remaining dough.

3. **PROOF:** Cover the pans with an overturned large plastic bin and set aside to proof in a warm (75°F), draft-free spot until the dough has doubled in volume, 3½ to 4 hours, and passes the Fingertip Test (page 76).

About 30 minutes before the loaves are finished proofing, position an oven rack in the center of the oven and preheat to 425°F.

4. **BAKE:** Whisk the egg in a small bowl, then brush generously all over the top of the loaves. Bake until mahogany, about 30 minutes, rotating the pans front to back halfway through. Transfer to a wire rack and let cool for 10 minutes in the pans before turning the loaves out onto the rack. Let cool completely before slicing and eating.

BRIOCHE BUNS

MAKES TWELVE 4-INCH BUNS

We use these for making Smoked Salmon Sliders (page 284) at the café or our PDA Burgers (page 330) at the restaurant, but they are delicious all on their own.

Basic Brioche Dough (page 164)   2 large eggs, for egg wash

1. MIX AND BULK FERMENT the brioche dough as directed.

2. DIVIDE AND SHAPE: Line two large baking sheets with parchment paper. Using a dough scraper, divide the dough into twelve 85-gram pieces.

Working with one piece of dough at a time, place it in the palm of your cupped hand and roll it around with your other cupped palm (as you would with Play-Doh) to form a smooth ball. Place it on one of the lined baking sheets, then continue shaping the remaining pieces of dough, spacing them 2 inches apart.

3. PROOF: Cover the baking sheets with an overturned plastic bin (if they don't fit, slide the parchment off the baking sheets and arrange so that they do fit, or use two containers) and let proof in a warm (75°F), draft-free spot until they have doubled in volume and pass the Fingertip Test (page 76), 3 to 3½ hours.

4. About 30 minutes before the buns have proofed completely, position two oven racks in the center of the oven and preheat to 425°F.

5. BAKE: Whisk the eggs in a small bowl, then brush each bun generously with the egg wash. Bake, rotating the pans front to back and between racks halfway through, until the buns are mahogany, 12 to 15 minutes.

6. COOL: Transfer the pans to a wire rack to cool for 10 minutes, then remove from the pans to cool completely.

SLIDER BUNS

MAKES ABOUT TWENTY-FOUR 2½-INCH BUNS

If you have three rimmed baking sheets and a roomy oven, you can bake these all at once. If not, place the last batch of 10 in the refrigerator to prevent them from over-proofing while the others bake.

Basic Brioche Dough (page 164)   2 large eggs, for egg wash

1. MIX AND BULK FERMENT the brioche dough as directed.

2. DIVIDE AND SHAPE: Line two or three baking sheets with parchment paper. With a dough scraper, divide the dough into twenty-four 34-gram pieces.

Working with one piece at a time, place it in the palm of your cupped hand and roll it around with your other cupped palm (as you would with Play-Doh) to form a smooth ball. Place it on one of the lined baking sheets, then continue shaping the remaining pieces of dough, spacing them 1½ inches apart.

3. PROOF: Cover the pans with an overturned plastic bin (if they don't fit, slide the parchment off the baking sheets and arrange so that they do fit, or use two bins) and let proof in a warm room-temperature (75°F), draft-free spot until they have doubled in volume and pass the Fingertip Test (page 76), 2½ to 3 hours. About 30 minutes before the buns have proofed completely, position two racks in the center of the oven and preheat to 425°F. Slide the buns on the parchment back onto the baking sheets and refrigerate one while the other two bake.

4. BAKE AND COOL: Whisk the eggs in a small bowl, then brush each bun generously with the egg wash. Bake until the buns are mahogany, 8 to 10 minutes, rotating the pans front to back and between racks halfway through. Transfer the pans to a wire rack to cool for 10 minutes, then remove from the pans to cool completely. Brush the remaining batch of buns with the egg wash. Bake and cool as above.

WALNUT STICKY BUNS

MAKES 12 STICKY BUNS

You will need a Texas muffin tin to make the bakery-size sticky buns we carry in our shops. Their sizes can vary, and this recipe works best with cups that are 3 inches wide and 2 inches deep. A 24-cup silicone version is available at www.jbprince.com and can easily be cut in half with kitchen scissors to make two smaller molds, each with 12 cups.

Basic Brioche Dough (page 164), chilled until firm (about 1 hour in freezer)

FOR THE PASTRY CREAM:

1 egg yolk

2 tablespoons granulated sugar

1 tablespoon all-purpose flour

1 teaspoon cornstarch

½ cup whole milk

FOR THE SCHMEAR:

2 sticks (8 ounces) unsalted butter, at room temperature (about 65°F)

¾ cup plus 2 tablespoons light brown sugar

¾ cup plus 2 tablespoons granulated sugar

1 teaspoon ground cinnamon

1 teaspoon fine sea salt

2 tablespoons heavy cream

FOR ASSEMBLY:

All-purpose flour, for dusting

200 grams finely chopped pecans or walnuts

Cooking spray, for the pan

1. **MIX AND BULK FERMENT** the brioche dough as directed.

2. **MAKE THE PASTRY CREAM:** In a medium bowl, whisk together the egg yolk, granulated sugar, flour, and cornstarch to form a paste.

In a saucepan, bring the milk to a boil over medium heat, watching carefully (it will bubble up very quickly and even more quickly bubble over). Remove from the heat and slowly pour half of the milk into the egg mixture, whisking until smooth (this tempers the egg yolk). Put the saucepan with the remaining milk back over medium heat and whisk in the paste (push it through a sieve with a spoon if it is lumpy). Bring the mixture to a boil, whisking constantly to prevent it from burning. Be careful—it will form big bubbles that may splash over when they burst. Cook until the paste is thick enough to coat the back of a spoon, about 1 minute; when you make a line on the spoon with your finger, it will remain there.

Remove from the heat and transfer the pastry cream to a bowl; cover the surface directly with plastic wrap to prevent a skin from forming. Cover the bowl tightly with another piece of plastic wrap and refrigerate the pastry cream until ready to use, up to 2 days.

RECIPE CONTINUES

3. MAKE THE SCHMEAR: In a stand mixer fitted with the paddle attachment, beat the butter, both sugars, cinnamon, and salt on medium speed, scraping down the bowl occasionally, until the mixture is smooth, about 2 minutes.

Turn the mixer to low and add the heavy cream in a slow stream. Continue to mix until the cream is thoroughly combined. Set aside.

4. TO ASSEMBLE: Lightly dust a work surface with flour. Roll out the chilled brioche dough to a 15 × 14-inch rectangle (it should be slightly thicker than ⅛ inch). With a long side facing you, spread one-third of the schmear onto the dough, spreading all the way to the edges with your knife (or offset spatula). Spoon the pastry cream on top of the schmear and spread it out to the edges to cover the schmear completely. Sprinkle half of the nuts evenly over the pastry cream.

5. SHAPE: Beginning at the long side closest to you, roll the dough onto itself as you would a carpet; you should end up with a 15-inch-long log. If the dough has become too soft to cleanly slice, refrigerate it for 30 minutes to firm it up. With a serrated knife, cut the log crosswise into 1¼-inch-wide rounds (about 100 grams each), using a sawing motion to avoid tearing the dough.

6. PROOF: Mist 12 cups of a Texas muffin tin with cooking spray. Use a small scoop to scoop about 2 tablespoons of the remaining schmear into each cup of the muffin tin. Divide the remaining nuts evenly among the cups. Place a round of dough, cut-side up, in each cup. Place an overturned plastic bin over the muffin tin and set aside to proof in a warm room-temperature (75°F), draft-free spot until the dough rises above the tin and passes the Fingertip Test (page 76), 1½ to 2 hours.

7. About 30 minutes before the buns have proofed completely, position a rack in the center of the oven and preheat to 375°F.

8. BAKE: Place a piece of parchment over the muffin tin, tamping it down so that it sits directly on the buns. Bake until the buns are deep brown and the interior dough is golden (slide a knife in between the spirals and gently pull away to check), 35 to 45 minutes, rotating the pan front to back halfway through.

9. COOL: Immediately after removing the buns from the oven, set an overturned tray on top of the tin, then flip the whole thing over. Let it sit for a few minutes—but not too long or the buns will stick (the cooked sugar acts like an adhesive). Carefully lift up the muffin tin (the melted butter and sugar will be very hot!) and put the tray on a cooling rack. Let cool long enough so that the buns don't burn your tongue!

Jose Guzman,

Head of Production, New York City

I grew up in Cuenca, a small town in Ecuador, where my grandfather owned a tiny bakery. My father worked in the bakery while my mother sold food (that my grandmother made) on a street corner in town. We lived in a room with a stone floor and a single bed for three people. Our lives changed when my grandfather punctured his leg on a nail at the bakery. At first, it seemed like nothing, but eventually, he required surgery or he would have lost his leg. He had to sell the bakery to pay the medical bills. That's when my dad and his brothers decided to come to the US—to help give my grandfather a better life. They flew to Mexico and swam across the Rio Grande. Not long after, my mother knew that she needed to also go to the States to give us a better life; she would send for us eventually. When she left, I pretty much lived with my grandfather, and my sister lived with my other grand-parents. So we were all separated. The only good thing to come out of that was that he taught me how to bake bread. My mother figured out how to get me to the States with an uncle; I pretended I was his son (my cousin), who actually already had a passport. I had to memorize all of the details from it and had to remind myself to answer to his name and write it down on any papers I was required to sign. On our direct flight to New York, the attendant handed out the customs declaration card, which required a signature. I was so nervous that I signed my own name. My uncle saved me by spilling soda on the paper and asking the atten-dant for another one. At immigration at JFK, we were pulled aside and asked to wait for what seemed like years. When the officer returned with our passports, he said he just wanted to make sure everything was in order. We ran through the doors of the airport to find my mother and father waiting with tears of joy. I hadn't seen my father in eight years, my mother in three. I was nine years old.

It was hard being a teenage immigrant. I found high school so challenging. I was placed in English-speaking classes from the beginning even though I didn't speak the language, so I learned a lot within a year.

I got my job at the bakery through my uncle Raul, who worked here. I eventually found out that he was my grandfather's favorite worker. He taught him everything he knew, and then, Raul was teaching me everything he knows. My first job was cleaning the trays and preparing the tools and equipment for the bakers. Eventually, I shaped the breads, and then became head of production, which involves dealing with multiple personalities! Now my whole family—here and in Ecuador—bakes. Even my wife works at Pain d'Avignon.

It is wonderful that I learn new things every day. When I was a kid, I wanted to be a cop because I loved *Robocop*. But baking was in my blood. And I'm so glad for that.

VIENNOI

and

OTHER

SWEETS

SERIES

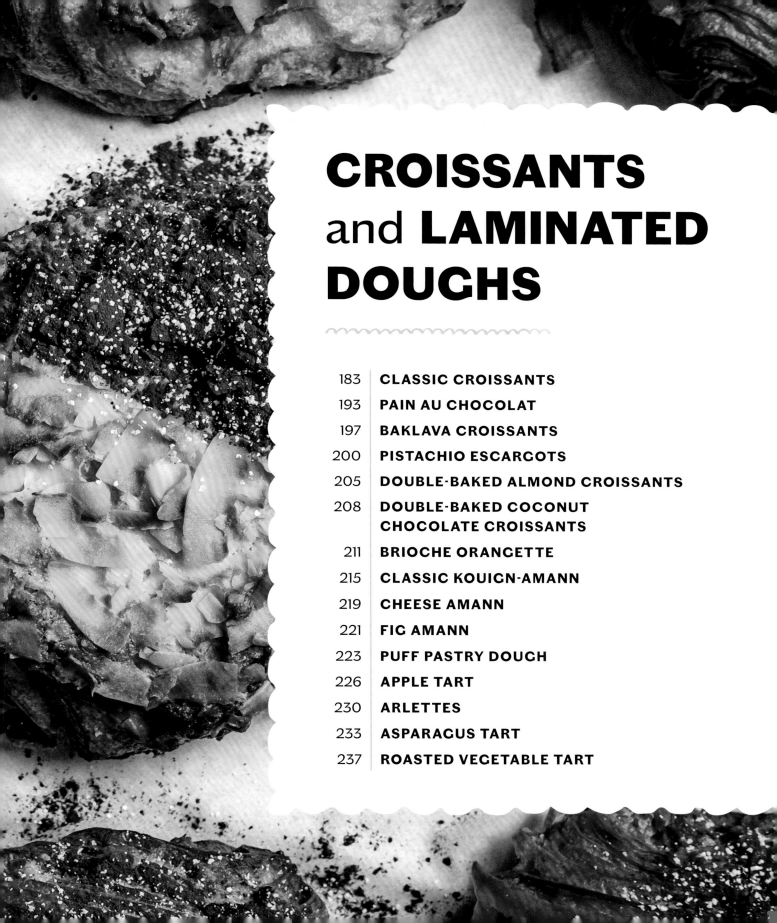

CROISSANTS and LAMINATED DOUGHS

We grew up eating *kifla*, a pastry native to central and eastern Europe, and an ancestor of the croissant, which, the story goes, dates back to fifteenth-century Austria, when the magnificent city of Vienna was besieged by the Ottoman Empire. The assault was launched at night, when presumably the city slept—except for its bakers, who were able to report on the incoming intrusion. To celebrate, the bakers made a moon-shaped pastry and the croissant was born.

There are few things in life that make me as excited to wake up in the morning as a good croissant. The closest thing to perfection I ever tasted was in the ski town of Val Thorens in the French Alps. After dropping Nika off at her ski school, I would stop by the local bakery. The dry air and zero humidity at this altitude made the croissant so crisp, its crust would crack without any resistance when I bit into it, and without crumbling to pieces. What's more, it wasn't greasy at all. I could eat it with my bare hands and it left no grease on my fingers, despite being loaded with butter, which was discernible by its uneven *alvéolage*, or honeycombing, created by the layers of butter separating the leaves of dough.

The process of making viennoiseries is not that different from the process of making bread. You will need to mix the dough, bulk ferment it, divide it, shape it, proof it, and bake it. Similarly, we use pre-ferments to improve the flavor, the aroma, the texture, and the color of our croissants. We like them to be light and airy with an uneven honeycomb crumb and without any noticeable acidic flavor. The crust should be super thin with a variety of shades between burnt orange and golden brown. Our pre-ferment of choice is poolish (see page 135), which helps us get those results. Even though the name of the croissant suggests that it should be crescent shaped, we like ours shaped straight.

The main difference between the bread-making process and the making of croissants is adding butter to the dough after the bulk fermentation has been completed. The actual step of enclosing the block of butter into a dough, or laminating it, is called *beurrage*. As a rule of thumb, the amount of butter incorporated is usually between one-quarter and one-third of the total dough weight. If you have 1 kilogram of dough, you will need between 250 and 330 grams of butter. The dough is flattened and rolled into a rectangle and the butter incorporated into the dough as if slipping a page into a book. Once you have created this, you will start rolling it out until it has stretched to three or four times its original size. You will then start folding the dough, multiplying the layers of butter and dough. This process is called lamination. Besides the multiplying of the butter layers, lamination reinforces the dough the same way folding the dough does during the bulk fermentation step in bread baking. In this section, we have provided detailed steps to successfully making viennoiseries the way our pastry chef, Francoise Ip, does every day.

LAMINATED DOUGHS

Laminated doughs—those in which blocks of butter are "folded" into yeasted doughs—are a labor of love. But they are certainly worth the effort when the results are shatteringly crisp croissants and *kouign-amann*. There are a few essential things to consider that will ensure your hard work will pay off: Use butter with 83% butterfat and a good-quality flour with a protein content between 11% and 12%, and avoid shortcuts around proper lamination of the dough.

Nice lamination can be achieved by using butter and dough that are the same consistency, which doesn't mean they will be the same temperature. If the dough gets too warm, it will begin proofing, it will be softer than the butter, and the lamination won't take. A cool kitchen, along with a cool work surface such as marble, is ideal. Working quickly, too, will ensure that the butter block does not get too warm and the dough does not over-proof. Keep in mind that the minute you mix the dough, it begins to proof.

There are several methods for laminating dough; we use the "book method," which is carried out exactly as you might imagine.

CLASSIC CROISSANTS

MAKES 12 CROISSANTS

FOR THE DOUGH:

522 grams all-purpose flour, plus more for dusting

75 grams sugar

12 grams fine sea salt

13 grams unsalted butter, cut into small pieces, at room temperature (about 65°F)

86 grams cold water (45°F)

162 grams Poolish (page 135)

50 grams (6 tablespoons) active dry yeast

113 grams whole milk

16 grams wildflower honey

FOR THE BUTTER BLOCK:

308 grams unsalted butter, preferably high-fat European-style (such as Plugra or Beurremont), at room temperature (about 65°F)

FOR THE EGG WASH:

2 large eggs

Whole milk

1. MIX THE DOUGH: In the bowl of a stand mixer fitted with the dough hook, combine the flour, sugar, and salt. Scatter the butter pieces over the dry ingredients. Set aside. In a separate bowl, combine the water, poolish, yeast, milk, and honey. Use your hands to dissolve the poolish in the liquid, squeezing it by the fistful until it is mostly dissolved. Pour the wet mixture into the flour mixture and mix the dough with your hands until it appears shaggy (the flour will not be entirely absorbed). Mix on low speed until the flour is completely absorbed. Increase the speed to medium-high and mix for about 3 minutes; it should be firm and smooth on the outside and reveal large holes in the center if you slice into it and pull it apart. (Take care not to overmix the dough.)

2. KNEAD, BULK FERMENT, STRETCH, AND FOLD: Remove the dough from the bowl and onto a clean work surface. Press the dough with your palms into a rough rectangle 1 inch thick, with a long side facing you. Pick up the dough and gently stretch it between your hands. Flip it over and turn it 90 degrees, so that a short side is now facing you. Push the top third of the dough away from you with the palm of your hand (this is the stretching), then roll the dough from the top onto itself toward you, using your thumbs to push firmly along the seam while resting your palms on top without pressing down on the dough. You should end up with a piece of log-shaped dough. Continue kneading this way until the dough is smooth and elastic, about 10 minutes. If the dough begins to stick to the work surface, dust it sparingly with flour.

Shape the dough into a smooth ball and return it to the bowl. Press a piece of plastic wrap directly onto the surface of the dough and set aside to proof in a warm (75°F), draft-free spot until it doubles in volume, 1½ to 2 hours, and passes the Windowpane Test (page 81).

RECIPE CONTINUES

Gently punch down on the dough in the bowl to deflate it. Lightly dust a work surface with flour and turn the dough out onto it. Press into a 7-inch square. Wrap the dough in a double layer of plastic and refrigerate overnight.

3. **MAKE THE BUTTER BLOCK:** Cut a 12 × 18-inch piece of parchment paper and lay it on a work surface. Fold it in half crosswise, then using a ruler, measure 7 inches from the fold and crease the parchment parallel to the fold. Fold the right side of the rectangle at the 2-inch mark, then use the ruler to measure 7 inches across. Crease the parchment here, and fold along the left side. You should have a 7-inch square. Open up the parchment and put the butter in the center of the square. Fold the parchment along the creases to make a secure packet. Using a rolling pin, roll the butter out to the corners of the packet, making sure it forms an evenly thick square. Refrigerate until the butter is thoroughly chilled, 30 to 60 minutes. It should be firm, not malleable.

4. **PREPARE THE DOUGH AND BUTTER FOR LAMINATION:** Fill a sheet pan with ice or ice packs and set it on a work surface to chill the surface before you set the dough on it.

Transfer the dough from the refrigerator to the freezer for 15 to 20 minutes to firm it up; its temperature should register about 36°F. Test by pressing your thumb into it; it should leave an impression but require force to do so, and the dough should not bounce back. At the same time, transfer the butter block to the countertop to sit for 5 to 10 minutes; the butter is the right consistency when it is slightly malleable, and you can fold it in half without cracking or breaking it. If it is too soft, refrigerate it until it reaches that malleable consistency.

5. **LAMINATE THE DOUGH:** Remove the pan of ice from the work surface. Place the dough on the chilled surface, and with the palms of your hands, press it into a rectangle of even thickness, with a short side facing you. Position a rolling pin parallel to the edge of the work surface and roll out; begin in the middle and roll up, then return to the middle and roll down. Repeat rolling out the dough this way until it measures 14 × 7 inches. Cut the dough in half crosswise. Place the butter block on one of the halves, and then place the other half on top of the butter, aligning the edges. Lightly dust the work surface with flour. With a cut side of the dough packet parallel to the edge of the work surface, use the rolling pin to lightly tap out the dough, beginning in the middle and working to the top, then returning to the middle and tapping to the bottom. (The even tapping helps ensure that all the butter doesn't shift to one side of the dough.) Continue to roll and tap out the dough until it measures 21 × 7 inches; it should be a little less than ½ inch thick.

6. **SINGLE FOLD:** Brush any excess flour off the surface of the dough. Mark the dough evenly into three sections by measuring and marking the edge lightly with a sharp knife every 7 inches along a long side of the dough. Fold the dough into thirds at the imaginary lines: from the bottom third to the middle, followed by the top third to cover it, making sure the edges are aligned. (If there is a buckle, the butter won't laminate properly.) Turn the dough

90 degrees so that the folded edge is either on your left or your right. Tap gently with the rolling pin as above and gently roll away from you to make a 10 × 7-inch rectangle. Wrap in plastic and freeze until the dough packet is firm, 20 to 30 minutes, checking periodically to make sure the butter doesn't get so cold that it becomes brittle (this can cause it to break through the layers and make it difficult to roll out).

7. DOUBLE FOLD: Lightly dust a work surface with flour and place the dough packet on it, with a short side parallel to the edge of the work surface. Use the rolling pin to lightly tap out the dough, beginning in the middle and working to the top, then returning to the middle and tapping down. After tapping on the dough back and forth three times, flip the dough over and repeat the process, rolling out the dough until it measures 28 × 7 inches. As you roll it out, lift the dough gently with your hands to keep it from sticking to the work surface and to ensure that it's of even thickness. (Lightly dust the work surface with flour if the dough is sticking.) Brush any excess flour off the dough. Turn the dough 90 degrees so that a long side is parallel with the edge of the work surface. Eyeball an imaginary vertical line down the middle of the dough. Fold the dough, this time by lifting the left side to the right, passing the imaginary center line by about 1 inch. Then bring the right side to meet it; the meeting point will be off-center. Make sure to do this all the while aligning the edges. Keeping the meeting point off-center ensures that the gap between the two sides will stay closed while stretching. Fold the dough onto itself as if closing a book. Lightly tap the dough, beginning in the middle and working to the top, then returning to the middle and tapping to the bottom. Continue

RECIPE CONTINUES

tapping until you have a 14 × 7-inch rectangle, with a short side parallel to the edge of the work surface. Cut the dough in half to make two 7-inch squares. Wrap both squares in plastic and refrigerate for 30 minutes.

8. **ROLL OUT THE DOUGH:** Fill a sheet pan with ice or ice packs and set it on a work surface to chill the surface. Work with one sheet of dough at a time (keep the second sheet refrigerated until it is ready to roll out). Lightly dust the work surface with flour and place a sheet of dough on it, with the cut side parallel to the work surface. With the rolling pin, gently tap the dough, working from the middle to the top and then from the middle to the bottom. Flip the dough over and tap with the rolling pin until the dough is ¼ inch thick and measures 10 × 7 inches. Wrap in plastic and refrigerate for 10 minutes to help the dough relax (rolling warms the dough, causing it to bounce back, which makes it difficult to roll to the desired length). Return the dough to the work surface with a short side parallel to the edge of the work surface. Roll the dough out to a 13 × 9-inch rectangle about ⅛ inch thick by rolling from the middle to the top, bottom, left, and right. Lift the dough as you work to prevent it from sticking to the surface and to gauge its overall thickness. With a sharp knife, trim the long edges and one short edge to make them neat. Rotate the dough 90 degrees so that a long side is parallel to the edge of the work surface.

9. **CUT THE DOUGH:** With a ruler and a single-edge razor blade, measure and mark along the bottom edge every 4 inches. Cut the dough crosswise at each 4-inch mark to make three

4 × 9-inch rectangles. Cut each piece in half diagonally to make 2 triangles. Roll out and cut the other half of the dough, for a total of 12 triangles.

10. SHAPE THE CROISSANTS: Line two half-sheet pans with parchment paper. Whisk one of the eggs with a splash of milk in a small bowl to make an egg wash.

Place a triangle of dough on the work surface, with the base closest to you. Working from the base, gently stretch the triangle until it measures 11 inches. Press the tip of the triangle into the work surface to ground it. Roll the dough up from the base to the tip, like a carpet that is 5 inches long and 2 inches wide at the center. Place on the sheet pan and repeat with the remaining triangles. Place the croissants on the prepared pans, spacing them 1½ to 2 inches apart. With your palm, gently press down on each croissant; this anchors them in place as you move the sheet pan around. Generously brush the croissants all over with the egg wash.

11. FINAL PROOF: Cover the sheet pans with overturned plastic bins and set aside to proof in a warm (75°F), draft-free spot until the croissants have doubled in volume and they jiggle a bit if you gently shake the pan, 2 to 3 hours. Gently squeeze the center of the croissant with your thumb and middle finger; the dough should feel relaxed and not resistant. If it feels like you could easily "pop" the croissant, it is over-proofed and will bake up big and fat. Refrigerate them for 10 to 15 minutes to allow the butter to firm up and thus help set the shape of the croissant.

About 30 minutes before the croissants have proofed completely, position two racks in the center of the oven and preheat to 400°F. Whisk the remaining egg with a splash of milk

RECIPE CONTINUES

in a small bowl. Very gently brush the croissants with the egg wash a second time, taking care not to deflate them.

12. **BAKE:** Bake for 10 minutes, then reduce the oven temperature to 375°F. Switch racks, rotating the sheet pans front to back, and continue baking until the croissants are deep golden, about 10 minutes more. If you give a croissant a light squeeze, it won't give, but if you press harder, it will shatter.

13. **COOL:** Transfer the pans to a wire rack to cool. Eat warm.

OOZING BUTTER?

Pools of butter on the baking sheet can mean a few things. One may be that your croissants are under-proofed. As a result, the dough won't expand enough in the oven, leaving the butter inside the croissant with nowhere to go. If the dough is properly proofed and butter still pools on the sheet, it may be that the butter and dough did not laminate well. This can happen if the butter is too cold when you are rolling out the dough, causing it to rip or crack the dough.

Francoise Ip,

Corporate Pastry Chef

In the 1980s and '90s, there was a big push in Hong Kong among my parents' generation to come West. More often than not, that meant the US. It was all about opportunity and education. It seemed like everyone in Hong Kong was applying for a green card.

It took me ten years to get one. There was the matter of sponsorship, which we had through my dad's brother and my mom's sister, both of whom were living here. For a full decade, my parents hoped and waited. I don't think I was all that aware—I was just a kid, living my life. In fact, I never really thought I would leave Hong Kong. The crazy thing is, word comes in a letter and it can come at any time.

I remember feeling pretty neutral about the whole thing: Not sad, not excited, although honestly a bit relieved. In Hong Kong, the year after you turn sixteen, you take a big, intense exam that determines where you go to college. The green card meant that I wasn't going to have to take it.

We traveled as a family to the US. My parents returned to Hong Kong shortly after to finish up their government jobs, and I lived with my aunt and uncle on Long Island. I was with a new family I didn't really know, in a new country, in a new house, and at a new school. I went to an English-speaking school in Hong Kong, so the language wasn't new to me. But it was a big adjustment to talk to people. I barely spoke outside of class. I was shy about making mistakes. I did meet a fair number of Asian-born Americans in high school, many of whom welcomed me into their homes. Some of their parents spoke Cantonese, so I felt right at home.

But I was lonely. So I returned to Hong Kong for the first half of my junior year, then returned to the US with my mom while my dad completed his work contract. I was fortunate to go to Cornell University, where I learned in ways far different than the rote memorization so traditional in Hong Kong. I learned how to apply concepts to real life. I loved everything about college, made lifelong friends, and coincidentally, I grew to love baking.

My older sister, who was in college in Canada, taught me how to bake cookies when I visited. I didn't grow up baking at all. In Hong Kong, only wealthy people have ovens in their homes. Middle-class families live in apartments that have super-tiny kitchens, with maybe a toaster oven. With my sister, I enjoyed the measuring and mixing immensely—so much so that I became the designated baker among my friends at school. I wound up baking all the time. I had no idea you could get a degree in it.

It is a cliché, but most Asian parents want their kids to pursue prestigious occupations—doctor, lawyer, architect. To tell my parents that I wanted to trade medical school for culinary school was not easy. They were very accepting, but I know deep down they were sad. I felt like I had disappointed them so much that I didn't talk to them for three months. I stayed in Ithaca for a year after I graduated and waitressed to save up to go to the New England Culinary Institute.

To this day, my parents still struggle with my decision—"You have to be on your feet every day," "You get burns!" But I don't plan on changing their minds; some beliefs are just too ingrained. I could never have become a professional baker if I hadn't come to the US. And I love the idea that one seemingly inconsequential experience—baking with my sister—became so consequential to my life.

PAIN AU CHOCOLAT

MAKES 12 PASTRIES

We use Valrhona chocolate in the shape of batons at the bakery, but any good-quality chocolate that is 70% cacao will work.

Dough for Classic Croissants (page 183)

All-purpose flour, for dusting

3 large eggs, for egg wash

432 grams dark chocolate (70% cacao), very finely chopped (or 24 Valrhona chocolate batons)

1. Make the dough for the croissants through step 7. After the dough has been refrigerated for 30 minutes, place one sheet on a lightly floured work surface, with the fold parallel to the edge. (Keep the second sheet refrigerated until ready to cut out.)

2. ROLL OUT THE DOUGH: Fill a sheet pan with ice or ice packs and set it on a work surface to chill the surface. Lightly dust the surface with flour and place one square of dough on it, with the cut side parallel to the edge. Refrigerate the second sheet of dough until ready to use. With the rolling pin, gently tap the dough, working from the middle to the top and then from the middle to the bottom. Flip the dough over and continue to tap with the rolling pin until the dough is ¼ inch thick and measures 10 × 7 inches. Wrap in plastic and refrigerate for 10 minutes to help the dough relax (rolling warms the dough, causing it to bounce back and making it difficult to roll to the desired length). Return the dough to the lightly floured work surface, with a short side parallel to the edge of the work surface. Continue rolling from the middle in all directions, top, bottom, left, and right, until you yield a 13 × 14-inch rectangle about ⅛ inch thick. The shorter edge should be parallel to the edge of the work surface. Lift the dough as you work to prevent it from sticking to the surface and to gauge its overall thickness. Rotate the dough 90 degrees so that the longer edge is parallel to the edge of the work surface.

3. CUT THE DOUGH: Using a sharp knife, trim away ½ inch from each edge. With a ruler and a single-edge razor blade, cut the dough in half lengthwise, yielding two 6 × 13-inch rectangles. Score the dough every 3¼ inches along the bottom edge (long side), then cut the dough crosswise to make 6 rectangles, each measuring 3¼ × 6 inches. Repeat the rolling and cutting with the other half of the dough.

RECIPE CONTINUES

4. SHAPE THE PASTRIES: Line two baking sheets with parchment paper. In a small bowl, whisk the eggs together for the egg wash. Place a rectangle of dough on the work surface with a short side facing you. Scatter 1 tablespoon of the chocolate (or 1 Valrhona chocolate baton) in a line about ½ inch from the bottom edge. Fold the dough over the chocolate to the halfway point of the rectangle. Scatter another tablespoon of the chocolate (or a second baton) in the same manner in the middle of the folded half, then roll up the dough onto itself, finishing with the seam side down. Gently press on the top of the pastry with your palm to prevent the dough from unraveling in the proofing stage. Repeat with the remaining rectangles of dough and space them 2 inches apart. Brush with the egg wash.

5. FINAL PROOF: Cover the baking sheets with overturned plastic bins and proof the pastries in a warm (75°F), draft-free spot until doubled in volume, 2 to 3 hours. They should jiggle if you gently shake the pan. About 30 minutes before the pastries have proofed completely, position two racks in the center of the oven and preheat to 400°F. Very gently brush the croissants with egg wash a second time, taking care not to deflate them.

6. BAKE: Bake for 10 minutes, then reduce the oven temperature to 375°F. Switch racks, rotating the pans front to back, and bake until the pastries are deep golden, about 10 minutes more.

7. COOL: Transfer the pans to a wire rack to cool. If you can resist, let the pastries cool slightly before serving. Eat warm.

BAKLAVA CROISSANTS

MAKES 15 PASTRIES

Inspired by a recipe from Snežana's mother, these are exactly what their name suggests—walnut paste layered in between triangles of croissant dough, rather than the traditional phyllo dough, then drenched in vanilla syrup.

During my first year in the US, while Snežana was still in Belgrade, she used to send baklava she made herself to me whenever anyone we knew was flying from Belgrade to New York. Our baklava "mules" knew that they could get in trouble with customs by bringing these in, but they always took the risk to smuggle these sweet pieces of love.

At the bakery, we bake these in custom-made rings to give the pastry super-sharp edges. It isn't necessary—without the rings they will have a triangle shape and still all the goodness. Most of the elements of this involved croissant can be made ahead: the filling will keep, tightly covered, in the refrigerator up to 7 days; the confit lemons can be stored in their syrup until ready to use, and the simple syrup, too, can be made ahead and stored, tightly covered, until ready to use.

Dough for Classic Croissants (page 183)

2 eggs, beaten separately, for egg washes

Splash of whole milk

FOR THE WALNUT FILLING:

¾ cup sugar

1 stick (4 ounces) unsalted butter at room temperature

2½ teaspoons grated lemon zest

½ teaspoon kosher salt

1¼ cups walnut pieces, chopped finely

FOR THE CONFIT LEMONS:

2 lemons, cut crosswise into ⅛-inch-thick slices

2 cups sugar

2 cups water

FOR THE VANILLA SYRUP:

Scant 1 cup sugar

1 cup water

1 teaspoon vanilla paste

1. Make the dough for the croissants through step 7.

2. MAKE THE WALNUT FILLING: In a stand mixer fitted with the paddle attachment, mix the sugar, butter, lemon zest, and salt on medium speed until combined. Reduce the speed to low and add ¾ cup of the walnuts and mix until they are evenly distributed. Store tightly covered in the refrigerator until ready to use.

RECIPE CONTINUES

3. ROLL OUT AND CUT THE DOUGH: Follow the directions in step 2 of Pain au Chocolat (page 193) until the dough is rolled out to a 13 × 14-inch rectangle. Trim about ½ inch off all the edges. Using a ruler, score the dough along the short side at 4-inch intervals, then using the ruler as your guide, use a sharp knife to cut the dough into three 4 × 13-inch strips. Pick up the strips and stack them on top of each other to make one 4 × 13-inch-long strip. Along the top edge of the stack, score the dough at 4-inch intervals. Along the bottom edge of the stack, make one score mark 2 inches in from the left edge and after that every 4 inches. Cut the dough into triangles, making angled cuts beginning at the 2-inch score mark at the bottom and the 4-inch mark at the top. Next, make an angled cut from that same 4-inch mark on the top to the next score on the bottom. Continue in this way to cut out 15 triangles. Roll and cut the second piece of dough in the same fashion, for a total of 30 triangles.

4. SHAPE AND FILL: Line two sheet pans with parchment paper. Working with 6 triangles at a time (put the others in the refrigerator and pull them out as you go), place 2 tablespoons of the walnut filling in the center of each of 3 triangles and lightly press 1 teaspoon of the walnuts on top of each mound of paste. Brush all three edges of the triangles with egg wash, then top with another triangle, stretching them a little bit so that they cover the paste and the edges are flush. Press first on the three points of the triangles to seal, then press together around the sides. Arrange on the pans.

5. FINAL PROOF: Cover the pans with overturned plastic bins and set aside to proof in a warm (75°F), draft-free spot until the croissants have doubled in volume and jiggle a bit if you gently shake the pan, 1 to 1½ hours. Gently squeeze the center of the croissant with your

thumb and middle finger; the dough should feel relaxed and not resistant. If it feels like you could easily "pop" the croissant, it is over-proofed and will bake up big and flat. Refrigerate for 10 to 15 minutes to allow the butter to firm up, thus helping to set the shape of the pastry.

6. **MEANWHILE, MAKE THE CONFIT LEMONS:** Place the lemon slices in a pot of cold water and bring to a boil. Drain the water and repeat two more times to remove any bitterness from the pith and peel. In a small saucepan, combine the sugar and water. Add the lemon slices and bring the mixture to a simmer. Reduce the heat to low and simmer until the peels are tender, 1 hour. Using a slotted spoon, transfer the lemons to paper towels to drain off any excess syrup.

7. **BAKE:** About 30 minutes before the croissants have proofed completely, position two racks in the center of the oven and preheat to 400°F. In a small bowl, whisk the remaining egg with a splash of milk. Very gently brush the croissants with egg wash a second time, taking care not to deflate them. Place a lemon slice in the center of each one. Bake for 10 minutes, then reduce the oven temperature to 375°F. Switch racks, rotating the pans front to back, and bake until the croissants are deep golden, about 10 minutes more.

8. **MEANWHILE, MAKE THE VANILLA SYRUP:** In a small saucepan, combine the sugar and water and bring to a simmer. As soon as the liquid is clear, remove it from the heat. Stir in the vanilla paste.

9. **BRUSH THE PASTRIES:** As soon as the croissants come out of the oven, transfer the pans to a wire rack and brush the croissants with the vanilla syrup. Eat warm.

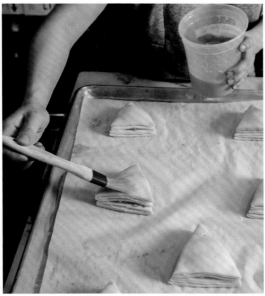

PISTACHIO ESCARGOTS

MAKES 16 PASTRIES

Dark chocolate and a delicious nut spread fill these spiral-shaped pastries, filled the way one would a jelly roll, then sliced crosswise.

Dough for Classic Croissants (page 183)

All-purpose flour, for dusting

3 large eggs, for egg wash

Pistachio Cream (page 203)

⅓ cup chopped (⅓-inch pieces) dark chocolate (70% cacao)

1. Make the dough for the croissants through step 7.

2. ROLL OUT THE DOUGH: Fill a sheet pan with ice or ice packs and set it on a work surface to chill the surface. Lightly dust the surface with flour and place one square of dough on it, with the cut side parallel to the edge. (Refrigerate the second sheet of dough until ready to use.) With the rolling pin, gently tap the dough, working from the middle to the top and then from the middle to the bottom. Flip the dough over and continue to tap with the rolling pin until the dough is ¼ inch thick and measures 12 × 7 inches. Wrap in plastic and refrigerate for 10 minutes to help the dough relax (rolling warms the dough, causing it to bounce back and making it difficult to roll to the desired length). Return the dough to the lightly floured work surface, with a short side parallel to the edge of the work surface. Roll out to a 10 × 17-inch rectangle by rolling from the middle to the top, bottom, left, and right. Lift the dough as you work to prevent it from sticking to the counter and to gauge its overall thickness.

3. FILL AND SHAPE THE PASTRIES: Line three baking sheets with parchment paper. In a small bowl, whisk the eggs together.

Using an offset spatula or dull knife, spread half of the pistachio cream all over the dough, leaving a 1-inch border along the top edge. Sprinkle half of the chocolate chunks evenly all over the cream. Working from the bottom, roll the dough up like a carpet. Press gently on the log, working from left to right, to keep it tight as you roll it up. As you approach the top edge, press it onto the work surface to "adhere" it. Continue rolling to the end, then press the seam firmly onto the log to prevent it from coming apart during the final proofing. Let the log chill in the freezer for about 30 minutes. With a sharp knife, trim the ends, then cut the roll into 1¼-inch-thick rounds to make 8 pastries. Place the rounds 6 inches apart on the baking sheets, then generously brush each with the egg wash.

Repeat the rolling, filling, and shaping with the other half of the dough.

RECIPE CONTINUES

4. FINAL PROOF: Cover the baking sheets with overturned plastic bins (slide the parchment off the pans and tuck all three sheets of parchment under the bins) and let the dough proof in a warm (75°F), draft-free spot until doubled in volume, 1½ to 2 hours. The spirals should jiggle if you gently shake the pan.

About 30 minutes before the dough has proofed completely, position three racks in the center of the oven and preheat to 400°F. (If you have only two oven racks, place one sheet pan of pastries in the refrigerator until ready to bake.) Very gently brush the pastries with the egg wash a second time, taking care not to deflate them.

5. BAKE: Bake for 10 minutes, then reduce the oven temperature to 375°F. Switch racks, rotating the pans from front to back, and bake until deep golden, 6 to 7 minutes more.

6. COOL: Transfer the pans to a wire rack to cool. Eat warm.

PISTACHIO CREAM

The cream will keep, tightly covered, in the refrigerator up to 5 days. To freeze, spoon into a 1-quart resealable plastic bag, seal, and press flat. Bring to room temperature before using. The cream will keep up to 1 month in the freezer.

Makes about 1½ cups

1½ sticks (6 ounces) unsalted butter, at room temperature
½ cup plus 2 tablespoons sugar
1 medium egg
¾ teaspoon vanilla paste or pure vanilla extract
¼ cup all-purpose flour
1⅓ cups finely chopped raw pistachio pieces

In a stand mixer fitted with the paddle attachment, mix the butter and sugar on medium speed until combined. With the mixer running, add the egg, mixing well to incorporate. Add the vanilla and let the paddle spin a few times. Turn the speed to low and add the flour and pistachios and mix until the cream is uniform.

DOUBLE-BAKED ALMOND CROISSANTS

MAKES 12 PASTRIES

We make these from day-old croissants and you should, too. They can be made from scratch, but the fresh croissant is so flaky and fragile that it doesn't slice as nicely as a next-day croissant. If you do make them from scratch, let the croissants cool completely and, of course, use a serrated knife to slice them open. The cake syrup (which is diluted simple syrup) is meant to add moisture more than sweetness. The filling can be made ahead and kept, covered tightly, in the refrigerator up to 3 days.

FOR THE ALMOND CREAM:

2 sticks (8 ounces) butter, at room temperature

1 cup granulated sugar

4 large eggs, whisked

1¾ teaspoons vanilla paste

1½ teaspoons almond extract

3¼ cups almond flour

½ cup plus 2 tablespoons all-purpose flour

FOR THE CAKE SYRUP:

¼ cup granulated sugar

1 cup hot water

FOR ASSEMBLY:

12 day-old croissants

¾ cup skin-on sliced almonds

2 tablespoons powdered sugar, optional

1. MAKE THE ALMOND CREAM: In a stand mixer fitted with the paddle attachment, mix the butter and sugar on medium speed until combined. Add the eggs in a slow stream until they are thoroughly blended. Add the vanilla paste and almond extract and let the paddle spin around a few more times. Reduce the speed to low and add both flours and mix until the mixture is creamy.

2. MAKE THE CAKE SYRUP: In a small bowl, whisk together the sugar and hot water until the sugar is dissolved.

3. ASSEMBLE AND BAKE: Preheat the oven to 325°F. Line a baking sheet with parchment paper or a silicone baking mat.

RECIPE CONTINUES

Using a serrated knife, slice the croissants in half horizontally and brush some of the syrup on both cut sides. Using a 2-ounce scoop, drop the almond cream on the bottom half of each croissant and spread evenly, then close each one up. Spread about 1 ounce (½ scoop) of almond cream on top of each croissant along its length. Sprinkle the almonds over the almond cream.

Transfer to the oven and bake until the almond cream is golden and the almonds are nicely toasted, 25 to 30 minutes. Let cool slightly, then tap the powdered sugar, if using, through a fine-mesh sieve over the tops. Eat warm.

DOUBLE-BAKED COCONUT CHOCOLATE CROISSANTS

MAKES 12 PASTRIES

It's not as though pain au chocolat needs anything more to recommend it, but why not a generous swipe of coconut almond cream? In the unlikely event you have any day-old pastries on your hands, these are as indulgent as it gets.

FOR THE COCONUT ALMOND CREAM:

2 sticks (8 ounces) butter, at room temperature

1 cup granulated sugar

3 large eggs, whisked

3 tablespoons coconut rum

1 teaspoon almond extract

1½ cups unsweetened coconut flakes or chips

1 cup plus 2½ tablespoons almond flour

¼ cup plus 3 tablespoons all-purpose flour

¾ cup white chocolate chunks

FOR THE CAKE SYRUP:

¼ cup granulated sugar

1 cup hot water

FOR ASSEMBLY:

12 day-old pains au chocolat

¾ cup unsweetened coconut flakes or chips, for sprinkling

Good-quality unsweetened cocoa powder, for dusting

Powdered sugar, for dusting

1. **MAKE THE COCONUT ALMOND CREAM:** In a stand mixer fitted with the paddle attachment, mix the butter and sugar on medium speed until combined. Add the eggs in a slow stream and mix until thoroughly blended. Add the coconut rum and almond extract and mix until there is no evidence of either. Reduce the speed to low, add the coconut flakes and both flours, and mix until they are thoroughly incorporated into the mixture. Add the white chocolate chunks and mix until distributed evenly in the cream.

2. **MAKE THE CAKE SYRUP:** In a small bowl, whisk together the sugar and hot water until the sugar is dissolved.

3. **ASSEMBLE AND BAKE:** Preheat the oven to 325°F. Line a baking sheet with parchment paper or a silicone baking mat.

Slice the pastries in half horizontally and brush some of the syrup on both cut sides. Using a 2-ounce scoop, drop the coconut almond cream onto the bottom half of each pastry, spread evenly, and then close each one up. Spread about 1 ounce (½ scoop) of the cream along the length of each pastry and place on the baking sheet. Sprinkle 1 tablespoon of the coconut flakes over each croissant. Place them ½ inch apart on the baking sheet.

RECIPE CONTINUES

DOUBLE-BAKED
ALMOND
CROISSANTS

DOUBLE-BAKED
COCONUT
CHOCOLATE
CROISSANTS

Transfer to the oven and bake until the coconut almond cream is golden and the coconut is nicely toasted, about 25 minutes.

4. COOL: Let cool for 30 minutes. Tap the cocoa powder through a fine-mesh sieve onto half of each croissant (use a piece of paper to cover the other half when you are doing the dusting). Gently tap the powdered sugar through a fine-mesh sieve over the cocoa. Eat warm.

BRIOCHE ORANGETTE

MAKES 12 PASTRIES

The inspiration for this pastry comes from northeastern Italy, the region we most frequently visited due to its proximity to Slovenia and Croatia. It is shaped like a croissant and filled with apricot jam and a touch of orange zest. Most brioche is not laminated, meaning there are no folded layers of butter. But this is one exception. The eggs and butter make this a heavier dough, so more kneading is necessary to strengthen it. To do this, mix the dough in a stand mixer and let the dough hook do the work.

FOR THE BRIOCHE DOUGH:

64 grams whole milk, heated until just warm to the touch

9 grams (3¼ teaspoons) active dry yeast

642 grams all-purpose flour, plus more for dusting

319 grams (about 6 large) eggs

94 grams sugar

39 grams finely grated orange zest

13 grams fine sea salt

124 grams unsalted butter, cut into ¼-inch pieces, at room temperature

FOR THE BUTTER BLOCK:

177 grams unsalted butter, preferably high-fat European style (such as Plugra or Beurremont), at room temperature (about 65°F)

FOR THE FILLING:

350 grams (1 cup plus 2 tablespoons) good-quality apricot jam

FOR THE EGG WASH:

2 large eggs

Splash of milk

1. Follow the directions for mixing Basic Brioche Dough (step 1, page 164), using the ingredient amounts listed here (make sure to add the orange zest and omit the pâte fermentée. Instead of using your hands to mix the dough, use a stand mixer fitted with a dough hook).

2. Follow steps 2 through 7 in Classic Croissants (page 183), using the butter block amount listed here.

3. ROLL OUT THE DOUGH: Line two baking sheets with parchment paper.

Fill a sheet pan with ice or ice packs and set it on a work surface to chill it. Lightly dust the surface with flour and place one square of dough on it, with the cut side parallel to the edge. Refrigerate the second sheet of dough until ready to use. With the rolling pin, gently tap the dough, working from the middle to the top and then from the middle to the bottom. Flip the dough over and continue to tap with the rolling pin until the dough is evenly ⅛ inch thick and measures 9 × 14 inches. Lift the dough as you work to prevent it from sticking to the counter and to gauge its overall thickness; you want it to be even. If the dough resists stretching, wrap it up and return it to the refrigerator until firm.

RECIPE CONTINUES

4. **CUT AND FILL:** Place the dough on the lightly floured work surface, with a short side parallel to the edge. Rolling from the middle to the top and then from the middle to the bottom, roll out a 10 × 28-inch rectangle. Lift the dough as you work to prevent it from sticking and to gauge its overall thickness.

Using a yardstick and either a pizza cutter, single-edge razor blade, or very sharp knife, trim ½ inch from all four sides of the dough, then cut it in half lengthwise to make two rectangles, each measuring 4½ × 13½ inches (you will need to use a steady hand when making that long cut). Cut each piece crosswise every 4½ inches to make a total of six 4½-inch squares. Roll out and cut the other half of the dough to yield 6 more squares. Working with one piece of dough at a time, spoon 1½ tablespoons of jam into the upper-left quadrant of the square. Fold the dough onto itself to create a triangle, bringing the bottom right corner over to the top left corner, letting it overlap by about ⅛ inch. (This allows for shrinkage of the top layer of the pastry.) Press firmly to close up the seam. Repeat with the remaining dough. Arrange the pastries on the prepared baking sheets, spacing them 1½ inches apart. Whisk together one of the eggs with a splash of milk and generously brush onto the pastries.

5. **FINAL PROOF:** Cover the pans with overturned plastic bins and set aside to proof in a warm (75°F), draft-free spot until the pastries have doubled in volume and jiggle a bit if you gently shake the pan, 1 to 1½ hours. Gently squeeze the center of the pastry with your thumb and middle finger; the dough should feel relaxed and not resistant. If it feels like you could easily "pop" the pastry, it is over-proofed and will bake up big and flat. Refrigerate for 10 to 15 minutes to allow the butter to firm up, and thus help set the shape of the pastry.

6. **BAKE:** About 30 minutes before the pastries have proofed completely, position two racks in the center of the oven and preheat to 400°F. Whisk together the remaining egg with a splash of milk. Generously brush the pastries with the egg wash. Transfer to the oven and bake for 10 minutes, then reduce the oven temperature to 375°F. Switch racks, rotating the pans front to back, and continue baking until the pastries are deep golden and crack a bit when pressed in the middle, 7 to 8 minutes more. If the pastries give easily when pressed, bake a few more minutes.

CLASSIC KOUIGN-AMANN

MAKES 10 TO 12 PASTRIES

These are simply muffin-shaped caramelized croissants in which you work the classic croissant dough through the double fold, then do two additional single folds.

At the bakery, we make *kouign-amann* from scraps of croissant dough run through a sheeter to mash them all together to achieve an even thickness. Only if you are on a baking spree might you find yourself with scraps, but in the event that you do, they will keep up to 2 days in the refrigerator and 1 week in the freezer. The day before you plan to use the scraps, remove them from the freezer and put them in the refrigerator. The final proofing for scraps is only 30 minutes, as it has already been partially proofed.

Use a 3 × 2-inch muffin tin (a.k.a. jumbo muffin tin, or Texas muffin tin; see page 170) to make these.

Dough for Classic Croissants (page 183)	All-purpose flour, for dusting 480 grams (2½ cups) sugar	Unsalted butter, at room temperature, for the muffin tin

1. Make the dough for the croissants through step 7 (the double fold), but do not cut the dough in half. Leave it whole.

2. SECOND SINGLE FOLD: Fill a sheet pan with ice or ice packs and set it on a work surface to chill the surface before you set the dough on it. Lightly dust the surface with flour and place the dough on it with the fold to your left or right. With the rolling pin, gently tap the dough, working from the middle to the top and then from the middle to the bottom. Flip the dough over and continue to tap with the rolling pin until the dough is 7 × 21 inches and just shy of ½ inch thick.

Brush any excess flour off the surface of the dough. Eyeball two horizontal lines to divide the dough into three equal sections. Fold the dough at the imaginary lines to make a 7 × 7-inch square, making sure the edges are aligned and flush; if there is a buckle, the butter won't laminate to the dough properly.

Turn the dough 90 degrees so that a folded side is to your left (or right) again, tap gently with the rolling pin as above, and gently roll out to make a 7 × 10-inch rectangle. Wrap in plastic and freeze until the dough packet is firm, 20 to 30 minutes, checking periodically to make sure the butter doesn't get too cold and become brittle (this can cause it to break through the layers and make it difficult to roll out).

RECIPE CONTINUES

3. THIRD SINGLE FOLD: Repeat the single fold as above. After rolling the dough out to a 7 × 21-inch rectangle, eyeball two horizontal lines that divide the dough into three equal sections.

Sprinkle 40 grams of the sugar evenly over the middle third of the dough. Fold the top third over the middle third (now halves), then sprinkle 40 more grams of the sugar evenly on top of this fold. Fold the bottom half onto the middle to make a 7-inch square. Be sure that the edges are flush. Wrap tightly in plastic wrap and refrigerate for 1 hour. (Alternatively, freeze the dough overnight and transfer to the refrigerator 3 hours before using.) In both scenarios, when you press the dough between your two fingers, it should no longer be hard.

4. CUT AND SHAPE: Fill a sheet pan with ice or ice packs and set it on a work surface to chill it.

Dust the work surface lightly with flour, then place the dough on it, with the fold parallel to the edge. With the rolling pin at a 90-degree angle to the edge of your work surface, roll the dough out to a rectangle ⅛ inch thick and about 10 × 18 inches, working from the middle to the right and then from the middle to the left. If the dough resists stretching, wrap it up and return it to the refrigerator until firm. Lift the dough as you work to prevent it from sticking to the surface and to gauge its overall thickness; you want it to be even.

With a long side parallel to the edge, press your index finger along the top of the dough to anchor it to the work surface. Sprinkle 100 grams of the sugar evenly over the dough, leaving a 1-inch border along the top edge (this bare border will help the dough seal properly).

Roll up the dough like a carpet, beginning on one end and tucking it tightly as you work across to the other end, taking care not to pull or stretch the dough.

Place the rolled dough seam-side down on the work surface. Trim the ends (you can use them to add to other pieces as necessary to make them all even). With a sharp knife, slice the roll crosswise into 1½- to 1¾-inch-thick rounds to yield 10 to 12 rounds.

Pour 200 grams of the sugar into a shallow bowl. Lightly rub 10 to 12 cups of a Texas muffin tin with the softened butter. Dredge each round of dough in the sugar, turning it over and onto its sides to coat completely. Place a round in each buttered cup, then press down gently so that the bottom sits flat.

5. FINAL PROOF: Cover the muffin tin with an overturned plastic bin and let the pastries proof in a warm (75°F), draft-free spot until the cups are three-quarters full, 30 to 45 minutes. (The empty spaces on the bottom of the cup will be filled in and the dough will come to within ⅛ inch of the sides of it.)

6. BAKE: Position a rack in the center of the oven and preheat the oven to 420°F.

Sprinkle the kouign-amann with the remaining 100 grams sugar, dividing evenly. Slide the muffin tin onto a baking sheet. Bake until the pastries are deep golden and the sugar is caramelized, 25 to 30 minutes, rotating the pan front to back halfway through.

Have a cooling rack ready—as soon as the kouign-amann come out of the oven, turn them out onto the rack (if they cool in the pan, the sugar will harden like crazy glue!). Eat warm.

7. STORE: Store the pastries in a resealable plastic bag. To crisp them up, place on a sheet pan and reheat in an oven at 400°F for 5 to 7 minutes. Avoid microwaving at all costs; it will just make them soft and limp.

CHEESE AMANN

MAKES 12 PASTRIES

As with the Classic Kouign-Amann (page 215), you will make a double fold followed by two single folds. The cheese is spread on the dough in the final single fold. Use a 3 × 2-inch muffin tin (a jumbo muffin tin or Texas muffin tin, page 170) for these.

Dough for Classic Croissants (page 183)

400 grams (14 ounces) Gruyère cheese, grated on the large holes of a box grater

1 teaspoon paprika

All-purpose flour, for dusting

Unsalted butter, at room temperature, for the muffin tin

128 grams (¾ cup) Seed Mix (page 221)

FOR THE EGG WASH:

1 large egg

Splash of milk

1. Make the dough for the croissants (page 183) through step 7 (the double fold).

2. SECOND SINGLE FOLD: Combine the Gruyère and paprika in a small bowl and set aside. Lightly dust a work surface with flour and place the dough on it, with the folded edge to your left or right. With the rolling pin, gently tap the dough, working from the middle to the top and then from the middle to the bottom. Flip the dough over and continue to tap with the rolling pin until the dough is 7 × 21 inches and just shy of ½ inch thick. Brush any excess flour off the surface of the dough. Eyeball two horizontal lines to divide the dough into three equal sections. Fold the dough into thirds at the imaginary lines from the top third to the middle followed by the bottom third on top of it, making sure the edges are aligned and flush; if there is a buckle, the butter won't laminate to the dough properly.

Turn the dough 90 degrees so that the new folded side is again to your left or right. Tap gently with the rolling pin as above, and gently roll out a 7 × 10-inch rectangle. Wrap in plastic wrap and freeze until the dough packet is firm, 20 to 30 minutes, checking periodically to make sure the butter doesn't get too cold and become brittle (this can cause it to break through the layers and make it difficult to roll out).

3. THIRD SINGLE FOLD: Repeat the single fold as above. After rolling the dough out to a 7 × 21-inch rectangle, mark it at 7-inch intervals along a long side to divide it into three sections.

RECIPE CONTINUES

Sprinkle 80 grams of the Gruyère mixture evenly on the middle third of the dough. Fold the top third over the middle third, then sprinkle another 80 grams of the Gruyère mixture over, and fold the bottom half over it to make a 7-inch square. Be sure that the edges are flush. Wrap tightly in plastic wrap and refrigerate for 1 hour.

4. CUT AND SHAPE: Coat 12 cups of a Texas muffin tin with softened butter. Put 1 tablespoon of the seed mix on the bottom of each cup.

Fill a sheet pan with ice or ice packs and set it on a work surface to chill it.

Dust the work surface with flour and place the dough on it, with the fold parallel to the edge. Lightly dust the dough with flour. With the rolling pin at a 90-degree angle to the dough, and working from the middle to the right, left, top, and bottom, roll out a 15 × 19-inch rectangle about ⅛ inch thick, with the long side parallel to the edge of the work surface. If the dough resists stretching, wrap it up and return it to the refrigerator. Lift the dough as you work to prevent it from sticking to the counter and to gauge its overall thickness.

With a yardstick and a pizza cutter, a single-edge razor blade, or a very sharp knife, trim about ½ inch from all four sides, then cut the dough lengthwise into 3 rows each measuring about 4½ inches wide. Along a long side of each strip, mark off every 4½ inches with a knife and cut crosswise to make twelve 4½-inch squares.

Working with one square at a time, put 20 grams of the Gruyère mixture in the center of each square. Bring the four corners up around it and pinch them together. Press the packages into the prepared muffin cups.

5. FINAL PROOF: Cover the muffin tin with a kitchen towel and let the pastries proof in a warm (75°F), draft-free spot for 30 to 45 minutes. (The empty spaces on the bottom of each cup will be filled in and the dough will come to within ⅛ inch of the sides of it.)

6. BAKE: Meanwhile, preheat the oven to 375°F. Whisk the egg with a splash of milk in a small bowl to make the egg wash.

Brush the proofed pastries with the egg wash, then sprinkle the remaining seed mixture over each, dividing evenly. Bake until the pastries are deep golden, 25 to 28 minutes, rotating the pan halfway through. Turn the pastries out onto a wire rack immediately. Eat warm.

7. STORE: Store the pastries in a resealable plastic bag. To crisp them up, place on a sheet pan and reheat in an oven at 400°F for 5 to 7 minutes. Avoid microwaving at all costs; it will just make them soft and limp.

SEED MIX

Makes 256 grams (about 1½ cups)

24 grams sesame seeds

48 grams flaxseeds

24 grams caraway seeds

80 grams sunflower seeds

80 grams poppy seeds

Mix the seeds together in an airtight container and refrigerate until ready to use.

VARIATION: FIG AMANN

Follow the directions for Cheese Amann (page 219), omitting the Gruyère and paprika and using 1½ tablespoons fig jam, 2 tablespoons soft goat cheese, and a quartered fresh Black Mission fig to fill each square. Brush the pastries with the egg wash and sprinkle evenly with flaky salt, such as Maldon, and black sesame seeds or seed mix. Bake and cool as directed.

PUFF PASTRY

Puff pastry is a lovely neutral dough that is as at home in a sweet as it is in a savory. It is somewhat easier to work with than croissant dough because it doesn't contain any yeast. However, there are a few things to keep in mind as you work with puff pastry:

- Tapping the dough before rolling helps to laminate the butter to the dough and reduces your chances of breaking the butter when rolling it out.

- Use flour sparingly when rolling out the dough and dusting the work surface; too much flour will dry out the dough and cause it to crack.

- On every fold, make sure the edges are flush with each other; this ensures everything made with the dough has an equal number of layers.

- Because puff pastry dough gets one extra turn, it gets tighter and benefits from an overnight rest in the refrigerator. Wrap in plastic wrap and refrigerate at least 8 hours or overnight.

- Puff pastry takes well to freezing; you can make a big block of dough, roll it out into sheets, freeze it, let it thaw, roll it out, and bake it off.

TO FREEZE: Roll out the puff pastry into the shape you want, wrap it in two layers of plastic wrap, and freeze for up to 1 month. Be sure to wrap it tightly; if it is exposed to air, it will crack when you roll it out. If using the sheet as is, you can take it straight from the freezer and put it right into the oven. If you need to fold it or manipulate it (as in Arlettes, page 230), let it thaw until it is somewhat bendable.

PUFF PASTRY DOUGH

MAKES TWO 12 × 18-INCH SHEETS, ENOUGH FOR TWO 12 × 16-INCH TARTS

You will note that we fold the dough off-center for the final fold because if the edges meet in the center and you fold the dough in half, there can be a gap and the lamination will not occur.

FOR THE BUTTER BLOCK:

360 grams unsalted butter, preferably high-fat European-style (such as Plugra or Beurremont), at room temperature (about 65°F)

FOR THE DOUGH:

862 grams all-purpose flour, plus more for dusting

13 grams fine sea salt

408 grams cold water (40°F)

6 grams distilled white vinegar

16 grams unsalted butter, preferably high-fat European-style, at room temperature (about 65°F)

1. **MAKE THE BUTTER BLOCK:** Follow step 3 of Classic Croissants (page 183).

2. **MIX THE DOUGH:** In a stand mixer fitted with the dough hook, mix together the flour, salt, water, and vinegar on low speed until the dough comes together and there are no dry pieces. Increase the speed to medium-high, add the butter, and mix until the dough is uniform and you can pull on the dough without breaking it, 3 to 4 minutes.

Transfer the dough to a clean work surface and press down on it with your palms to make a disc ½ inch thick. Use a sharp knife to score the dough with a large X, then open the flaps (this reduces the chill time), wrap it in plastic wrap, and refrigerate 2 to 3 hours or overnight.

3. **PREPARE THE DOUGH AND BUTTER FOR LAMINATION:** Fill a sheet pan with ice or ice packs and set it on a work surface to chill it.

Transfer the dough from the refrigerator to the freezer for 15 to 20 minutes to firm it up; its temperature should register about 36°F. Test by pressing your thumb into it; it should leave an impression but require force to do so, and the dough should not bounce back. At the same time, transfer the butter block to the countertop to sit for 5 to 10 minutes; the butter is the right consistency when it is slightly malleable and you can "fold" it without breaking it. If it is too soft, refrigerate it until it passes this "bend test"; if it is too hard or shows small cracks along the edges, leave it out at room temperature for 5 to 10 minutes before pounding out.

4. **LAMINATE THE DOUGH:** Remove the sheet pan of ice from the work surface; wipe down the surface to remove any condensation from the pan. Place the dough on the work surface. With the palms of your hands, press the dough into an evenly thick rectangle, with a short side facing you. Roll the dough out into a rectangle, beginning in the middle and rolling

RECIPE CONTINUES

to the top, then returning to the middle and rolling to the bottom. Repeat until it measures 14½ × 7½ inches. Turn the dough 90 degrees so that the long side is parallel to the edge of the work surface.

Center the butter block on the left side. Fold the right "page" over it. Moisten your fingertips with a bit of water, then run them along the edges of the dough before sealing to help "glue" the seams. The butter will leak out if the seams are loose. Press the seams together with your thumb and forefinger to fully enclose the butter.

Lightly dust the work surface with flour. Lightly tap on the dough with the rolling pin, beginning in the middle and working to the top, then returning to the middle and tapping to the bottom. (The even tapping helps ensure that all the butter doesn't shift to one side within the dough.) Roll out the dough, tapping as needed until the rectangle measures 21 × 7 inches; it should be a little less than ½ inch thick. Rotate the dough 90 degrees so that the long side is parallel to the work surface.

5. SINGLE FOLD: Brush any excess flour off the surface of the dough. Visually divide the dough evenly into three sections by measuring and marking lightly with a tick every 7 inches across the length of the dough. Fold the dough into thirds at the imaginary lines, from the left third to the middle, followed by the right third to cover it, making sure the edges are aligned and flush. Wrap the dough in plastic and refrigerate for 30 minutes.

6. DOUBLE FOLD: Lightly dust a work surface with flour and place the dough packet on it, with the folded edge parallel to the edge of the work surface. With the rolling pin at a 90-degree angle to the edge of the work surface, lightly tap on the dough, beginning in the middle and working to the right; return to the middle, then tap along the dough to the left. Repeat tapping the dough three times, then flip the dough over and repeat. With the rolling pin at a 90-degree angle to the edge of the work surface, roll the dough into a 28 × 7-inch rectangle. As you roll it out, lift the dough gently to release it from the surface and ensure it is evenly thick. If the dough starts to stick, lightly dust the surface with flour.

Brush any excess flour off the dough. Eyeball a vertical line down the middle of the dough. Fold the dough, this time by lifting the left side to the right, passing the imaginary center line, and aligning the edges. Then bring the right side to meet it, so that the meeting point is off-center. Keeping the meeting point off-center ensures that the gap between the two sides will stay closed while rolling it out. Fold the dough in half as if closing a book, then turn it 90 degrees so that the fold is parallel to the edge of the work surface. With the rolling pin at a 90-degree angle to the edge of the work surface, lightly tap the dough, beginning in the middle and working to the right, then returning to the middle and working to the left. Tap and roll out to the left and right until you have a 14 × 7-inch rectangle, with a long side parallel to the edge of the work surface. Wrap the dough in plastic wrap and refrigerate for 1 hour.

7. **SECOND DOUBLE FOLD:** Fill a sheet pan with ice or ice packs and set it on a work surface to chill it. Follow step 6 opposite to give the dough a second double fold, rolling out the 14 × 7-inch rectangle to 28 × 7 inches. Wrap the dough in plastic and refrigerate for at least 8 hours or overnight.

8. **ROLL OUT THE DOUGH:** Lightly dust a work surface with flour. Divide the dough evenly into two pieces and roll each into a 12 × 18-inch sheet. If not using immediately, roll the dough up like a scroll, wrap in a double layer of plastic wrap, and refrigerate up to 3 days or freeze up to 1 month. Thaw for 2 hours in the refrigerator before using.

APPLE TART

MAKES ONE 10 × 16-INCH TART TO SERVE 10 TO 16

This is a classic French apple tart, made with an abundance of apples set into pastry cream and sprinkled with cinnamon sugar.

FOR THE PASTRY CREAM:

¾ cup whole milk

¼ cup sugar

2 large egg yolks (reserve whites for another use)

1 tablespoon unsalted butter, preferably high-fat European-style (such as Plugra or Beurremont)

1 tablespoon plus 2 teaspoons cornstarch

Pinch of fine sea salt

FOR THE TART:

1 sheet Puff Pastry Dough (page 223)

4 medium or 2 to 3 large Honeycrisp apples (Jonathans, Jonagolds, Granny Smith, and Braeburn are nice, too)

¼ cup sugar

¼ teaspoon ground cinnamon

2 tablespoons unsalted butter, melted

1. Line a quarter-sheet pan with plastic wrap.

2. MAKE THE PASTRY CREAM: In a saucepan, combine the milk, sugar, egg yolks, butter, cornstarch, and salt and bring to a boil over medium heat, whisking constantly. Continue boiling until the mixture reaches the consistency of pudding, about 1 minute (taste to be sure the "starchiness" of the cornstarch has been cooked out). Remove from the heat and spread the pastry cream onto the plastic wrap (it will stop cooking and cool faster). Press a second piece of plastic wrap directly onto the pastry cream to prevent a skin from forming. Let cool. The pastry cream will keep, with a piece of plastic wrap pressed onto its surface, in a tightly covered container for up to 5 days.

3. Position a rack in the center of the oven and preheat to 400°F. Line a half-sheet pan or rimmed baking sheet with parchment paper. Have a second sheet pan ready.

4. BAKE THE PASTRY: Place the 12 × 18-inch sheet of puff pastry dough on the lined sheet pan. Using a sharp knife, trim the dough as necessary to fit the pan. With a fork, pierce the dough all over. Place a piece of parchment paper over the dough and set the second baking sheet directly on top of it and bake until golden brown, 20 to 30 minutes, rotating the pan front to back halfway through. Transfer the pan to a wire rack, remove the top sheet pan, and let the pastry cool to room temperature (you don't want the pastry cream to "melt" as you brush it on the pastry). Leave the oven on and raise the heat to 425°F.

RECIPE CONTINUES

5. **ASSEMBLE THE TART:** Core and halve the apples, leaving the peel on them. Using a sharp knife or a mandoline, cut the apples into slices ⅛ inch thick.

Spread the pastry cream evenly across the entire sheet of cooled puff pastry. Arrange the apple slices in rows, shingle-style, over the cream, working from left to right along the length of the dough. Overlap the rows by about ⅛ inch; the apples shrink during baking and this overlap will prevent gaps between the rows.

In a small bowl, combine the sugar and cinnamon. Brush the apples evenly with the melted butter, then sprinkle the cinnamon sugar over them.

6. **BAKE:** Bake until the tart is golden brown and a fork slides easily into the apples, 25 to 30 minutes, rotating the pan front to back halfway through.

7. **COOL:** Transfer the tart to a wire rack to cool, then cut into squares and serve warm. To reheat, warm in a preheated 425°F oven for 10 minutes.

ARLETTES

MAKES 12 PASTRIES

These flattened puff pastry coils, cousins to the French palmier, are layered with cinnamon sugar. To bake them all at once, you will need four half–sheet pans or baking sheets, two to arrange the arlettes on and two more to press on top of them to keep them flat while baking. If you have only two pans, bake them in two batches; freeze the second sheet of dough while the first batch bakes. Alternatively, bake one batch and freeze the remaining for another time. Place them in a rigid container, separated by sheets of parchment paper.

2 cups granulated sugar

2 teaspoons ground cinnamon

1 sheet Puff Pastry Dough (page 223)

Powdered sugar, for dusting

1. Position two racks in the center of the oven and preheat the oven to 425°F. Line two half-sheet pans with parchment paper.

2. In a small bowl, whisk together the sugar and cinnamon. Place a 12 × 18-inch sheet of dough on a clean work surface, with a short side facing you. Sprinkle ¾ cup of the cinnamon sugar evenly over the dough. Roll the dough into a log, beginning at a short side and tucking tightly as you roll. Using a sharp knife, slice the log crosswise into 1-inch-thick rounds.

3. Tuck the tail of each round on the underside. Dip both sides of each round into the remaining cinnamon-sugar mixture, then transfer to a work surface, tail side down. Roll each round into a 5½-inch circle about ⅛ inch thick. Each round should be of even thickness.

RECIPE CONTINUES

ROASTED VEGETABLE TART

MAKES ONE 10 × 16-INCH TART, ENOUGH TO SERVE 8

Thinly sliced plum tomatoes are our go-to for this very popular tart, but eggplant, bell peppers, and zucchini work here, too.

1 sheet Puff Pastry Dough (page 223)

12 ounces goat cheese, softened until spreadable

Shallot Vinaigrette (page 234)

8 ounces feta cheese, crumbled

8 to 10 plum tomatoes, cut into ⅛-inch-thick slices

Sea salt and freshly ground black pepper

2 cups packed baby arugula

¼ cup chopped chives

Good-quality olive oil, for drizzling

1. Preheat the oven to 425°F. Line a half-sheet pan or rimmed baking sheet with parchment paper. Have a second sheet pan ready.

2. Follow step 4 of the Apple Tart (page 226) for parbaking the puff pastry sheet. Leave the oven on.

3. ASSEMBLE THE TART: Using an offset spatula, spread the goat cheese evenly across the sheet of cooled puff pastry. Drizzle shallot vinaigrette evenly over the goat cheese and scatter the crumbled feta over. Arrange the tomato slices over the cheese, overlapping them slightly. Season with salt and pepper.

4. BAKE: Bake until the tomatoes are softened and roasted, about 20 minutes, rotating the sheet front to back halfway through.

5. COOL: Transfer to a wire rack to cool slightly, about 10 minutes. Garnish with the arugula, chives, and a drizzle of olive oil; season with salt and pepper. Cut into 8 slices and serve. To reheat, warm in a 425°F oven for 10 minutes.

QUICHES and GALETTES

PÂTE BRISÉE

MAKES ENOUGH FOR ONE 9-INCH TART OR QUICHE

A high ratio of butter to flour gives this dough its crumbly texture; try not to handle it too much or it will become tough. Don't be tempted to skip chilling the dough sufficiently; the crust behaves better when it is chilled and, like most of us, has had time to relax. It wouldn't hurt to double this recipe to make two crusts—one for now and one for later.

230 grams (2 cups) all-purpose flour

6 grams (½ teaspoon) kosher salt

154 grams (1 stick plus 3 tablespoons) cold unsalted butter, preferably high-fat European style (such as Plugra or Beurremont), cut into ½-inch cubes

120 ml (½ cup) ice water, or more as needed

1. In a large bowl, whisk together the flour and salt. Using a pastry cutter or two knives, cut in the butter until the mixture resembles coarse meal. Take care not to overmix. Add the ice water a few tablespoons at a time and mix the dough with your hands, gradually adding more water as the dough comes together. Too much mixing after you've added the water results in an overworked dough, which results in a tough crust. Test it by pinching a piece between your thumb and forefinger; if it stays together, stop mixing. If it crumbles, add more water gradually.

2. Turn the dough out onto a clean work surface and shape into a 1½-inch-thick disc. Double-wrap in plastic wrap and refrigerate for at least 8 hours or overnight. The dough can be made ahead at this point and refrigerated up to 3 days or frozen for up to 1 month. If frozen, thaw the dough on the countertop for 15 to 20 minutes before proceeding with the recipe.

QUICHE CRUST

MAKES ONE 9-INCH CRUST

We use pastry rings at the bakery, but there's no reason you can't take the homespun route and bake this in a pie plate or tart pan of the same size.

Pâte Brisée (opposite)   Neutral oil, for the pan   All-purpose flour, for dusting

1. Make and chill the dough as directed.

2. Lightly coat a 9 × 2-inch ring mold, tart pan, or pie plate with a neutral oil. If using a ring mold, set it on a parchment paper–lined baking sheet.

3. Generously dust a work surface with flour and place the disc of dough on it. Give it a few whacks with your rolling pin, working from left to right, to soften it up a bit. Lightly dust the top of the dough with flour and roll it out, working from the middle and rotating the dough 90 degrees a few times in between rolls. Lift the dough and run it through your hands to make sure it is of even thickness. Roll out into a 12-inch disc.

4. Roll the dough back onto the pin, then center the pin at the back of the mold, tart pan, or pie plate and unroll the dough like a carpet over and into it. Using your index finger, press the dough firmly into the edge of the vessel where the sides meet the bottom. If using a ring mold or tart pan, trim away the excess dough. If using a pie plate, pinch the dough around the rim to make a lip that overhangs by ½ inch into the pie plate, then flute the edges by interlocking your thumbs and index fingers, working your way around the rim. Snip a little of the excess dough off and set the scraps aside; you may need it to patch the crust if it splits apart while baking. Refrigerate the dough until it is rock-hard, 30 minutes to 1 hour.

5. While the dough chills, position a rack in the center of the oven and preheat to 375°F.

6. Place a piece of parchment over the dough and fill it with pie weights, dried beans, rice, or salt. Bake until light golden, 20 to 25 minutes.

QUICHE
AMÉRICAINE

QUICHE
LORRAINE

QUICHE AMÉRICAINE

MAKES ONE 9-INCH ROUND QUICHE, ENOUGH TO SERVE 8

This is a hearty, hearty quiche—loaded with meat and cheese. One slice is a meal. We make these square at the café, but you can make them round like a pie at home.

Quiche Crust (page 241)

Quiche Custard (below)

8 chives, minced

¾ pound ham, cut into ½-inch pieces (about 1½ cups)

¾ pound sliced turkey, cut into ½-inch pieces (about 1½ cups)

6 ounces cheddar cheese, coarsely grated (about 1½ cups)

1. Bake the crust as directed, remove from the oven, and reduce the oven temperature to 350°F.

2. If the crust was baked in a ring mold, put the mold on a sheet pan. Pour enough custard into the crust to come three-quarters of the way up the sides. Scatter the chives, ham, turkey, and cheddar over it, then pour the remaining custard over the fillings.

3. Bake the quiche until the top is golden and the custard is firm and set (the center should not jiggle when the pan is gently shaken), about 50 minutes, rotating the pan from front to back halfway through.

4. Transfer the pan to a wire rack and let it cool at least 10 minutes before slicing and serving. The quiche will keep, tightly wrapped, in the refrigerator up to 5 days and up to 2 weeks in the freezer. To rewarm, wrap in foil and put in a preheated 350°F oven for 10 to 15 minutes.

QUICHE CUSTARD

The ratio of cream to egg is higher than what is standard, but this results in a richer filling and a cut that is smooth and clean—no oozing!

Makes enough for a 9-inch quiche

6 large eggs, preferably organic

2 cups half-and-half

¾ teaspoon salt

Pinch of freshly ground black pepper

Pinch of freshly ground nutmeg

In a large, deep bowl, whisk the eggs until the yolks and whites are well combined and the mixture is pale yellow. Add the half-and-half, salt, pepper, and nutmeg and whisk until frothy.

QUICHE LORRAINE

MAKES ONE 9-INCH ROUND QUICHE, ENOUGH TO SERVE 8

At the store in the famed Plaza Hotel, we sell out of quiche every day. When we were designing the menu, it seemed very natural to put this classic version on it.

Quiche Crust (page 241)

Quiche Custard (page 243)

1 cup grated Comté or cheddar cheese

¾ pound bacon, cooked and chopped

1 small shallot, thinly sliced into rings

1. Bake the crust as directed, remove from the oven, and reduce the oven temperature to 350°F.

2. If the crust was baked in a ring mold, put the mold on a sheet pan. Pour enough custard into the crust to come three-quarters of the way up the sides of the crust. Scatter the cheese, bacon, and shallot over the custard, then pour the remaining custard over the fillings.

3. Bake the quiche until the top is golden and the custard is firm and set (the center should not jiggle when the pan is gently shaken), about 50 minutes, rotating the pan front to back halfway through.

4. Transfer the quiche to a wire rack and let it cool at least 10 minutes before slicing and serving. The quiche will keep, tightly wrapped, in the refrigerator up to 5 days and up to 2 weeks in the freezer. To rewarm, wrap in foil and put in a preheated 350°F oven for 10 to 15 minutes.

TOMATO RICOTTA OLIVE QUICHE

MAKES ONE 9-INCH ROUND QUICHE, ENOUGH TO SERVE 8

The beauty of quiche is its chameleon-like custard; it can accept a host of varying ingredients to easily change its flavor profile. Here, the best of Italy, in a pie.

Quiche Crust (page 241)

2 cups grape tomatoes, halved

2 teaspoons good-quality olive oil

Pinch of kosher salt

1 cup whole-milk ricotta cheese

1 cup Kalamata olives, pitted and roughly chopped

¼ cup mixed soft fresh herbs you have on hand (chives, parsley, tarragon)

Quiche Custard (page 243)

1. Bake the crust as directed, remove from the oven, and reduce the oven temperature to 350°F. While the crust bakes, roast the tomatoes. Place on a half-sheet pan and toss with the olive oil. Season with the salt. Roast until the tomatoes have shriveled and browned around the edges, 10 to 15 minutes.

2. If the crust was baked in a ring mold, put the mold on a sheet pan. Spoon the ricotta cheese in 1-tablespoon portions into the shell. Scatter the tomatoes, olives, and herbs all over. Pour the custard over to fill.

3. Bake the quiche until the top is golden and the custard is firm and set (the center should not jiggle when the pan is gently shaken), about 50 minutes, rotating the pan front to back halfway through.

4. Transfer the quiche to a wire rack and let it cool at least 10 minutes before slicing and serving. The quiche will keep, tightly wrapped, in the refrigerator up to 5 days and up to 2 weeks in the freezer. To rewarm, wrap in foil and put in a preheated 350°F oven for 10 to 15 minutes.

SPINACH AND FETA QUICHE WITH CURRANTS AND ALMONDS

MAKES ONE 9-INCH ROUND QUICHE, ENOUGH TO SERVE 8

The aroma of lemon zest and nutmeg in the custard fills the room as this bakes, yet its flavor is ever so subtle. We serve a square version of this quiche at the café but share a round variation below.

Quiche Crust (page 241)

5 cups fresh spinach leaves

1½ cups crumbled feta cheese

¼ cup dried currants

¼ cup sliced almonds

¼ cup finely chopped soft herbs (chives, parsley, tarragon)

Grated zest of 1 lemon

Quiche Custard (page 243)

1. Bake the crust as directed, remove from the oven, and reduce the oven temperature to 350°F.

2. If the crust was baked in a ring mold, put the mold on a sheet pan. Scatter the spinach, feta, currants, almonds, herbs, and lemon zest all over the shell. Pour the custard over the fillings.

3. Bake the quiche until the top is golden and the custard is firm and set (the center should not jiggle when the pan is gently shaken), about 50 minutes, rotating the pan front to back halfway through.

4. Transfer the pan to a wire rack and let cool at least 10 minutes before slicing and serving. The quiche will keep, tightly wrapped, in the refrigerator up to 5 days and up to 2 weeks in the freezer. To rewarm, wrap in foil and put in a preheated 350°F oven for 10 to 15 minutes.

PLUM GALETTE WITH PISTACHIO CREAM

SERVES 6 TO 8

This is an informal, fun little pastry with a free-form crust that you can shape in all manner of ways. We use the index-finger method to form the pleats. At the bakery, we arrange the plum wedges in concentric circles, which gives the galette a polished look, but it tastes just as good when the slices are haphazardly piled over the cream.

Pâte Brisée (page 240)

All-purpose flour, for dusting

1 cup Pistachio Cream (page 203)

Grated zest of 1 lemon

4 to 5 plums, halved and cut into 1-inch wedges

1 large egg, lightly beaten

2 teaspoons sliced almonds

2 teaspoons organic cane sugar

1. Make and chill the dough as directed. The pastry is ready to roll out if it is slightly malleable; otherwise it will crack when you roll it out. Set it on the counter until your thumb just barely makes an impression in the center. Line a half-sheet pan with parchment paper. Dust a work surface with flour and sprinkle a bit of flour on the top of the disc of dough. Roll it out until it's around the thickness of a tortilla, about ⅛ inch thick, pushing the pin from the middle of the dough outward and turning the disc every few rolls. Don't worry if the edges are a bit ragged and uneven. Gently lift the dough and place it on the parchment-lined sheet pan.

2. Position a rack in the center of the oven and preheat the oven to 375°F.

3. Spread the pistachio cream onto the dough, leaving a 1-inch border around the edges uncovered. Sprinkle the lemon zest all over the cream. Arrange the plums over the cream, leaving a 1-inch border of cream exposed. Fold the edge of the dough onto the filling, pleating it as you go.

4. Brush the egg wash onto the crust, making sure to coat the nooks and crannies, then scatter the almonds over the fruit. Sprinkle the sugar all over the galette.

5. Bake until the edges are lightly browned (or as browned as you like—we like our crusts fairly dark) and the dough stays firm when you slide a spatula underneath the galette, 30 to 35 minutes.

6. The galette is best served warm. It will keep, covered, for 2 days.

SAVORY GALETTE VARIATIONS

HAM AND GRUYÈRE GALETTE

Spread the dough with ⅓ cup crème fraîche mixed with 1 tablespoon Dijon mustard, then layer 1 cup caramelized onions, ½ cup diced ham, and 1 cup grated Gruyère cheese, in that order.

HERBED TOMATO AND RICOTTA GALETTE

Spread ½ cup whipped ricotta cheese over the dough and top with roasted tomatoes (as many as you like) and chopped soft herbs (ditto).

ROASTED BUTTERNUT SQUASH GALETTE WITH CARAMELIZED ONIONS AND GRUYÈRE

Preheat the oven to 400°F. Peel and seed a 1-pound butternut squash. Cut into half-moons, drizzle with olive oil, and season with salt and freshly ground black pepper. Roast about 25 minutes. Arrange the squash over the dough, top with ½ cup caramelized red onions, 1 cup grated Gruyère cheese, and 1 teaspoon fresh thyme. Season with flaky salt.

HERBED TOMATO
AND RICOTTA
CALETTE

HAM AND
CRUYÈRE
CALETTE

ROASTED
BUTTERNUT SQUASH
CALETTE WITH
CARAMELIZED
ONIONS AND
CRUYÈRE

COFFEE & TEA

ESPRESSO		3
AMERICANO		3
MACCHIATO		3.50
CORTADO		3.50
CAPPUCCINO		4
LATTE		4.50
MOCHA		5
VANILLA LATTE		4.95
CHAI		4.50
DRIP COFFEE	2.25	2.50
TEA		2.75
COLD BREW	3.50	4.25
HOT CHOCOLATE		4.95
ALMOND, SOY, OAT		+0.50

STUMPTOWN
PROUDLY
SERVING
COFFEE

BEST BAGUETTE
NEW YORK 2018

VIGNON

SCONES, CAKES, a **COOKIE,** and an **EXCELLENT GRANOLA**

In the spring of 1999, just a few months before Tole and I moved to the Hamptons, we all went to Paris for the biggest baking convention in the world. We happened to stay at a little hotel on the Boulevard Saint-Germain right across the street from Café de Flore. Every morning we would cross the street and have our first morning coffee and croissant there. We enjoyed sitting at a table outside, watching people pass by. If there was anything we really missed in the US it was a good coffee and the outdoor cafés with waiter service, where no one would ask you to have a meal in order to sit down. Just a few hundred yards from the hotel there was a bakery where we could see the bakers working and baking bread through the window on the street. To us, it was like watching theater. This small bakery also resembled the bakeries back home, which made our hearts beat a little faster. To have our own retail store would be a dream come true. We wanted to put on that baking show in front of people. The project in the Hamptons was supposed to be exactly that. To have a retail shop was a dream that we never gave up on, and ten years later, we opened our first retail store. Today we have four.

Our first, at the Essex Market on the Lower East Side, is one of the last parts of Manhattan that feels like old-time New York. The market itself is home to a few produce purveyors, butchers, and fishmongers. Our space

was so small that only one employee fit behind the counter and only one customer could stand in front. Our second address was the legendary Plaza Hotel as part of a reinvention of their basement, which was previously occupied by fur and jewelry boutiques. The idea was to attract a younger crowd with a food hall, one of the first in the city, which was partially up and running by the time we arrived. We joined La Maison du Chocolat and François Payard and were followed by Ladurée, Luke's Lobster, and No. 7 Sub. Lady M, the famous Japanese maker of the finest pastries, also joined. To help us run things there, we were lucky to connect with Rosella Albanese, who had recently returned from Paris, where she worked in various bakeries. We shared a passion for the European heritage of communal interactions in which love and beauty are so often shared through food.

The kiosk at The Plaza was so small that we had to deliver breads and viennoiseries twice a day from the bakery. We did have room for a small oven in which to bake things like quiches, scones, galettes, and cakes. We also started offering sandwiches, soups, and salads. Our menu was rooted in the simplicity of our bread making. We would go weekly to the Union Square Market to buy fresh, seasonal produce, the same way our parents went to the greenmarkets in Belgrade.

In Belgrade, we all grew up in households where every day began with Turkish coffee. Neighbors would visit one another to have a coffee together. At every gathering, whether business or personal, coffee would be served. Every work break was a coffee break. And after every meal the coffee would follow. In other parts of the country where the style of life was under strong Italian influences, espresso was the coffee of choice. Whether stopping for a shot while standing at the espresso bar before work or sitting in a café sipping one afterward, the communal coffee experience was deeply ingrained in our DNA.

Coffee brings people together, the same way bread does. Our decision to add coffee to our repertoire was less business motivated and more Proustian, and we wanted the quality of our coffee to match the quality of our breads. As soon as we opened at The Plaza in 2012, the lines in front of our little store started forming and Café d'Avignon was born.

Most of the recipes that follow are Rosella's creations, inspired by our vision and guidance. We start with sweets that perfectly pair with a cup of coffee in the morning or the afternoon, and then continue with savory items more appropriate for a lunch or dinner. We hope you will have as much fun making and enjoying them as we do.

ON MAKING PERFECT SCONES

Making scones that check all the boxes—crumbly texture, tender crumb, and crisp crust—can be elusive, but there are a few techniques that can get you there.

It all begins with cold ingredients. Working with chilled butter results in a more tender crumb and helps build and maintain structural integrity—not totally dissimilar to biscuits. The same goes for the half-and-half. Take it straight from the refrigerator. If the kitchen is overly warm, working quickly and then chilling the scones in the fridge for 30 minutes or more before baking is an option.

To get that crumbly texture, take care not to overmix the dough. It should look like coarse gravel, not fine sand. You want to see chunks of butter in the mixture, but not so big that they melt and pool in the pan. The dough will feel dry and crumbly and won't fully stick together. When you dump it onto the work surface, it will look like it needs more handling to come together. Avoid this! Handle the dough as little as possible; you don't want to activate the gluten by forcing the liquids and proteins to "find" each other by way of overmixing or handling. Doing this will result in the creation of a gluten structure or network, which is great for bread but bad for scones. Overhandling can also result in warming the fats—which is not ideal. A tough scone will be the result.

We make round scones for our bakeries, but if you prefer the triangle shape, press the dough into a 4 × 12-inch rectangle (it should be about 1 inch thick). Using a dough scraper or sharp knife dipped in flour, cut 8 triangles along the length of the dough. Arrange on the baking sheet and proceed with the recipe.

BLUEBERRY LEMON SCONES

MAKES 8 SCONES

We use fresh blueberries to make our scones, but frozen blueberries will do if they are the only option available to you.

3½ cups all-purpose flour, plus more for dusting

⅓ cup sugar, plus more for dusting

2 tablespoons baking powder

½ teaspoon kosher salt

1½ sticks (6 ounces) cold butter, preferably high-fat European-style (such as Plugra or Beurremont), cut into ¼-inch cubes

1 cup half-and-half, plus more as needed

Grated zest of 1 lemon

2 to 2½ cups blueberries, preferably fresh

1 large egg, whisked

1. Position a rack in the upper third of the oven and preheat to 350°F. Line a half-sheet pan with parchment paper or a silicone baking mat.

2. In a large bowl, whisk together the flour, sugar, baking powder, and salt. Rub the cold butter cubes into the dry ingredients with your fingers, or use a plastic round-edged dough scraper or pastry cutter to cut the butter into the dry ingredients, working your way through the pieces until they are the size of pebbles. The mixture will resemble coarse sand and the butter will still be a bit chunky. Don't overmix!

3. In a small bowl, whisk together the half-and-half and lemon zest and pour it into the flour mixture. Use the dough scraper in a chopping motion to incorporate the liquid. Mix until the dough appears shaggy; add a few more tablespoons of half-and-half if necessary.

4. Fold the blueberries into the dough with the scraper, proceeding gently as you work your way around the bowl to avoid crushing the fruit.

5. Once the fruit is evenly distributed, dump the dough out onto the work surface (dust with flour only if the dough is sticky). Use the scraper to incorporate any loose flour into the dough, then press it into a 1½-inch-thick rectangle.

6. Dip a 3½-inch round biscuit cutter into a bit of flour to prevent the dough from sticking, then cut the scones out of the dough. Gather the scraps with your hands, handling gently, and turn the mass on its side and press into a 1½-inch-thick rectangle. Cut out the remaining scones. Arrange the scones about 1 inch apart on the sheet pan. Brush each scone with the whisked egg and dust with a bit of sugar.

7. Bake until the edges are browned and the center is golden, 25 to 30 minutes.

8. Put the sheet pan on a rack and let cool. Serve warm.

DARK CHOCOLATE SCONES

MAKES 8 SCONES

Chocolate with at least 70% cacao gives these scones just the right hint of bitterness; if you prefer an even higher cacao content, go for it. Serve these warm, perhaps with a smear of salted butter. Add a dollop of raspberry jam as well.

3¾ cups all-purpose flour, plus more for dusting

⅓ cup granulated sugar

2 tablespoons baking powder

½ teaspoon kosher salt

1½ sticks (6 ounces) cold unsalted butter, preferably high-fat European style (such as Plugra or Beurrement), cut into ½-inch cubes

1 cup half-and-half, plus more as needed

1 teaspoon vanilla paste

5.3 ounces dark chocolate (at least 70% cacao), cut into ½-inch chunks (about 1 cup)

1 large egg, whisked

2 teaspoons Vanilla Sugar (recipe follows), for dusting

1. Position a rack in the upper third of the oven and preheat to 350°F. Line a half-sheet pan with parchment paper or a silicone baking mat. Lightly flour a work surface.

2. Follow the directions in Blueberry Lemon Scones (page 263) but replace the blueberries and lemon zest with the vanilla paste and chocolate chunks.

3. Brush each scone with the whisked egg and sprinkle the tops with the vanilla sugar.

4. Bake until the edges are browned, the center is golden, and the sugar has formed a crackly, sparkling crust, 25 to 30 minutes.

5. Place the sheet pan on a rack and let cool. Serve warm.

VANILLA SUGAR

The better the quality of the fresh vanilla bean, the more intensely vanilla flavored the sugar. If you can find vanilla beans from Madagascar or Tahiti, by all means use them.

Makes 2 cups

1 vanilla bean pod, halved, seeds scraped and seeds and pod reserved
2 cups sugar

Place the seeds and the sugar, along with all of the sticky paste that came off on the scraping knife, into the bowl of a food processor and pulse until thoroughly blended and the seeds are broken up. Transfer to a jar with a tight-fitting lid. Cut up the pod, if necessary, so that it fits in the jar. Submerge the pieces in the sugar and cover tightly. Keep in a cool, dry place up to 2 months. The sugar is most flavorful after 2 weeks.

LEMON
BLUEBERRY
SCONES

DARK
CHOCOLATE
SCONES

BANANA
CREAM CHEESE
BREAD

CHOCOLATE
OLIVE OIL
CAKE

HONEY
CORNMEAL
CAKE

BANANA CREAM CHEESE BREAD

MAKES ONE 9 × 5-INCH LOAF

One of our most popular quick breads at the café, this is delicious with a good cup of coffee or tea at any time of day. Serve it warm, cut into thick slices.

⅓ cup canola oil, plus more for the pan

1⅓ cups all-purpose flour

1 teaspoon baking soda

¼ teaspoon kosher salt

¾ cup (6 ounces) cream cheese, at room temperature

½ cup packed dark brown sugar

3 tablespoons granulated sugar, plus more for sprinkling

3 bananas, 1 whole, and 2 roughly chopped

2 large eggs, lightly beaten

½ cup chocolate chips or walnuts (optional)

1. Preheat the oven to 325°F. Slick a 9 × 5-inch loaf pan with canola oil and line the pan with parchment paper long enough to come up the two long sides.

2. In a small bowl, whisk together the flour, baking soda, and salt.

3. In a stand mixer fitted with the paddle attachment, whip the cream cheese on medium speed until it is smooth, scraping down the bowl and paddle two or three times. Add both sugars and mix until well incorporated. Add the chopped bananas and mix until they are thoroughly broken up. Reduce the speed to low and add the eggs and oil in a slow stream. Mix until they are thoroughly incorporated. Gradually add the flour mixture and mix until thoroughly incorporated. Remove the bowl from the mixer and fold in the chocolate chips or walnuts, if using.

4. Using a rubber spatula, scrape the batter from the bowl into the prepared loaf pan and smooth the top with the back side of the spatula. Halve the remaining whole banana lengthwise and gently set the two halves on the top of the batter, cut-side up, as if they are interlocking in the center like the letter S. Sprinkle granulated sugar all over the top of the batter.

5. Bake until a cake tester inserted in the center comes out clean, 1 hour to 1 hour 10 minutes.

6. Cool in the pan on a wire rack for about 10 minutes. Slice into 1-inch-thick slices and serve.

HONEY CORNMEAL CAKE

MAKES ONE 9 × 5-INCH LOAF

This cake was born out of necessity; our store in The Plaza Hotel presented space challenges that made elaborate baking impossible. Bring on the simple dump-and-stir cake! This one is a delightful combination of lemon zest, honey, flaky salt, and cornmeal.

1 cup good-quality olive oil, plus more for the pan

1½ cups sugar

1⅓ cups plus 1 tablespoon all-purpose flour

¾ cup yellow cornmeal, fine to medium grind

1 teaspoon baking powder

½ teaspoon baking soda

½ teaspoon kosher salt

Grated zest of 2 lemons

1¼ cups whole milk

3 large eggs

⅓ cup honey

Hot water

Juice of 1 lemon

½ teaspoon flaky sea salt, such as Maldon

1. Preheat the oven to 350°F. Slick a 9 × 5-inch loaf pan with olive oil and line the pan with enough parchment paper to come up on the two long sides.

2. In a large bowl, whisk together the sugar, flour, cornmeal, baking powder, baking soda, salt, and half the lemon zest. Use the whisk to make a well in the center of the mixture.

3. In a small bowl, whisk together the milk, olive oil, and eggs. Pour into the well in the dry mixture and use the whisk to pull the dry ingredients into the wet, whisking through lumps and all the dry parts until the mixture is homogenous and the olive oil is no longer pooling. Scrape the batter from the bowl into the prepared loaf pan.

4. Bake until the top is lightly browned and a cake tester inserted in the center comes out clean, about 1 hour. Set the pan on a rack to let the cake cool, 7 to 10 minutes.

5. Meanwhile, in a spouted measuring cup, combine the honey with enough hot water to make ½ cup. Stir until the honey is melted. Stir in the lemon juice.

6. Use a dinner knife to make slits all over the surface of the cake, then pour the honey-lemon syrup all over the top while the cake is still warm. Sprinkle the salt and remaining lemon zest all over. Slice into 1-inch-thick slices and serve.

CHOCOLATE OLIVE OIL CAKE

MAKES ONE 9 × 5-INCH LOAF

Olive oil replaces butter in this super-moist cake, a customer favorite. This is another dump-and-stir cake, an ideal choice if space and time are at a premium.

1 cup good-quality mild extra-virgin olive oil, plus more for the pan

1¼ cups plus 2 tablespoons organic cane sugar

2 cups all-purpose flour

½ cup Dutch-process cocoa powder, plus more for dusting

½ teaspoon baking soda

½ teaspoon baking powder

½ teaspoon kosher salt

3 large eggs

1¼ cups whole milk

½ teaspoon vanilla paste

5 ounces dark chocolate (at least 70% cacao), chopped into ¼-inch shards

Flaky sea salt, such as Maldon, for sprinkling

1. Position a rack in the center of the oven and preheat the oven to 350°F. Slick a 9 × 5-inch loaf pan with olive oil and line the pan with enough parchment paper to come up on the two long sides.

2. Follow steps 2 and 3 of Honey Cornmeal Cake (opposite) to make the batter, substituting the cocoa powder for the cornmeal, omitting the lemon zest, and adding the vanilla paste in with the milk mixture. Fold the dark chocolate shards into the mixture. Scrape the batter into the prepared loaf pan.

3. Bake until a cake tester inserted in the center comes out clean and the center no longer jiggles, 1 hour 5 minutes to 1 hour 15 minutes.

4. Place the pan on a cooling rack to cool. When the loaf has cooled completely, tap some cocoa powder through a fine-mesh sieve all over the top, followed by a sprinkle of sea salt. Slice into 1-inch-thick slices and serve.

BLUEBERRY WAFFLE CAKE

SERVES 10 TO 12

This is made in one of those Bundt pans that looks like an exploded three-dimensional spirograph. It's called the Jubilee Bundt Pan (available at Williams-Sonoma and Amazon), though we call this a waffle cake because of its familiar squares. Of course, this cake can be made in a classic Bundt pan as well.

Canola oil spray, for the pan

2 cups all-purpose flour, plus more for the pan

2¼ teaspoons baking powder

1 teaspoon kosher salt

2 sticks (8 ounces) unsalted butter, preferably high-fat European-style (such as Plugra or Beurremont), at room temperature

1⅔ cups organic cane sugar

Grated zest of 1 lemon

3 large eggs

¾ cup whole milk

1 teaspoon vanilla paste

3 cups (about 14 ounces) blueberries, preferably fresh

Powdered sugar, for dusting

1. Position a rack in the center of the oven and preheat the oven to 350°F. Mist a Bundt pan with canola spray, then coat it all over with flour by tapping it through a sieve into the pan. Tap out the excess.

2. In a small bowl, whisk together the flour, baking powder, and salt.

3. In a stand mixer fitted with the paddle attachment, mix the butter, cane sugar, and lemon zest on medium-high speed until the mixture is pale yellow and fluffy, about 10 minutes, scraping down the bowl periodically. Reduce the speed to medium and add the eggs one at a time, beating well after each addition, again scraping down the bowl as needed. Add the milk and vanilla and mix until there's no visible trace of either. Turn off the mixer, add the flour mixture, and run the mixer on low until the flour is just combined.

4. Remove the bowl from the mixer and gently fold in the blueberries with a rubber spatula. Pour the batter into the prepared pan.

5. Bake until the top of the cake is deeply browned and a cake tester inserted in the center comes out clean, about 1 hour 10 minutes.

6. Put the pan on a rack to cool for 5 to 10 minutes. When the cake is still slightly warm, remove it from the pan. Gently turn the pan on its side and tap it all the way around on the countertop to help loosen it. Put an overturned plate over the pan and flip the cake out onto it. Let it cool completely, then tap a tablespoon or two of powdered sugar through a sieve all over the top of the cake.

CRANBERRY PECAN COOKIES

MAKES 16 COOKIES

Perhaps we were inspired by our sourdough loaf, but whatever the case, the combination of cranberries and pecans is one we love. These slice-and-bake cookies are shortbread-like in spirit, yet with a middle made soft by the cream cheese. They're an excellent accompaniment to a cup of coffee.

2 sticks (8 ounces) plus 1½ tablespoons unsalted butter, preferably high-fat European-style (such as Plugra or Beurremont), at room temperature

¼ cup (2 ounces) cream cheese, at room temperature

¾ cup sugar

¼ teaspoon vanilla paste

2 cups plus 2 tablespoons all-purpose flour

¾ teaspoon kosher salt

⅔ cup unsweetened dried cranberries

4 cups pecans, finely chopped

1. Position two racks in the center of the oven and preheat the oven to 300°F. Line two baking sheets with parchment paper or silicone baking mats.

2. In a stand mixer fitted with the paddle attachment, mix the butter, cream cheese, sugar, and vanilla on medium speed until the mixture is smooth. Reduce the speed to low and add the flour and salt, mixing until incorporated. Add the cranberries and mix until they are well distributed throughout the dough, about 1 minute.

3. Turn the dough out onto a clean work surface and roll into a 2¾-inch-thick log (about 16 inches long). Spread the pecans out on the work surface and roll the log in them until it is entirely coated. Cut the log crosswise into 1-inch-thick coins. Arrange on the baking sheets, about 1 inch apart.

4. Bake until the cookies turn golden brown around the edges, 25 to 30 minutes, switching racks and rotating the pans front to back halfway through. Transfer to a rack to cool for 15 minutes.

SEEDS AND NUTS GRANOLA

MAKES 7 TO 8 CUPS

This honey-sweetened granola recipe is infinitely malleable; just swap out the seeds and nuts called for with others based on your preferences. Use currants or raisins instead of cranberries; swap out the walnuts and almonds for pistachios and pecans. Add unsweetened coconut chips (about ½ cup) to the mix and/or give it added crunch and an omega boost with a few tablespoons of chia seeds.

This is marvelous with ice-cold milk, full-fat Greek yogurt, or, truthfully, entirely on its own, eaten by the handful.

Cooking spray

270 grams (3 cups) rolled oats

100 grams (1 cup) sliced almonds

100 grams (1 cup) walnut halves

130 grams (1 cup) sunflower seeds

10 grams (1 tablespoon) poppy seeds

10 grams (1 tablespoon) sesame seeds

4 grams (1 teaspoon) kosher salt

2 grams (½ teaspoon) ground cinnamon

4 grams (½ teaspoon) light brown sugar

105 grams (½ cup) good-quality olive oil

100 grams (½ cup) honey

75 grams (½ cup) dried cranberries

1. Preheat the oven to 325°F. Line a sheet pan with parchment paper and mist the paper with cooking spray.

2. In a large bowl, combine the oats, almonds, walnuts, sunflower seeds, poppy seeds, sesame seeds, salt, cinnamon, brown sugar, olive oil, and honey. Mix thoroughly until the ingredients are evenly distributed and all of the oats are coated in the olive oil and honey. Use your hands to toss and massage the liquids into the dry ingredients. Spread the mixture out onto the prepared pan.

3. Bake until the granola is golden, fragrant, and browned, 25 to 30 minutes. Every 10 minutes during baking, turn the granola over with a large spoon to allow it to toast evenly.

4. Put the pan on a rack to cool and once it has, sprinkle the cranberries over the top and toss to combine. The granola will keep in a tightly covered container at room temperature for 7 to 10 days.

Rosella Albanese,
Director of Retail Operations

I am a first-generation American, the daughter of Italian immigrants who came to the States in the 1960s. Both my mother, Rosa, and father, Antonio, are from Calabria, from the mountains and coast, respectively. My mom grew up in a village that looks a lot like *Game of Thrones*— stone houses, terra-cotta roofs, and cement floors. She stopped going to school when she was very young.

My dad was in the Italian navy. He jumped ship in Norfolk, Virginia, after a cook on board told him not to stay in the navy forever. He called a cousin in Massachusetts and never looked back. My mother made it to New York the traditional way, after waiting ten years for the proper papers. She was sixteen.

My parents met when my dad visited New York with a friend who knew my mom's grandfather. It turns out my mom knew my dad's mother. They used to wash clothes in the same river in their small town in Calabria! It is a classic story, really. They met and were married not long after, and eventually had my four brothers and sisters and me.

Our lives revolved around food. We had a huge garden with tomatoes, peppers, onions, squash blossoms, string beans, zucchini—you name it. At the end of every summer, we had an epic tomato sauce–making weekend—three families chopping, pureeing, and filling the jars that had been sterilized in a giant cauldron over a firepit my dad would build. Our hands were shriveled beyond recognition from peeling hundreds of tomatoes.

Sundays meant big family gatherings and pasta lunches, a tradition we continue to this day. My dad made wine in the basement from the grapes that he grew, as does my brother now. Family and friends would never show up at our house without something in hand that they had made. One cousin pickled eggplants, another made charcuterie, an uncle made grappa, and my great-grandmother made jam from grapes she grew over a trellis in her backyard. One of my aunts made her own soap.

You never left our house without some kind of food to take home. One year, my mother had a huge vat of my uncle's olive oil shipped over from Italy. Before any guest could leave, she would run down to the basement and ladle the olive oil into a container and tuck it into their bag as if it were contraband.

My mom was the kind of cook who wasted nothing. I have great memories of drinking a big bowl of sugar-sweetened cappuccino with chunks of rock-hard bread floating in it. It was like sophisticated cereal. Her espresso zabaglione is Proustian: That espresso with a whipped egg yolk folded into it, served in a demitasse, takes me right back to the kitchen table of my childhood.

I was not an immigrant, but being the child of immigrants had its challenges. Assimilating took the form of pleading for school lunches of PB&J on Wonder Bread instead of mortadella on home-baked country bread. And then there were those times friends came over for dinner and oily fish was on the menu. As we got older, Velveeta macaroni and cheese, scalloped potatoes, and sloppy joes began to creep into our lives. We just wanted what our friends were eating!

My parents were always *doing.* They always had so many projects going—most of them involving food. I love that about them. And I guess I am just like that, too. But more important, they taught me what it means to appreciate where I come from, to be proud of my culture, and to preserve the traditions they hold so dear. Working at the bakery with people from all over the world, essentially pursuing the same dream that my parents had, I feel right at home.

SIMPLE SANDWICHES

We wouldn't be a proper French bakery without trays filled with small sand-wiches, each one wrapped in white parchment, ready to be eaten out of hand. It's safe to say any filling will taste good between slices of bread you've baked yourself—here are some customer favorites.

TURKEY CLUB SANDWICH

MAKES 1 SANDWICH

This single-decker version of the classic quickly became a bestseller at our café. Roasted turkey on rye caraway bread makes a delicious combination; add as much crispy bacon, juicy tomato, and avocado as you want to top it off.

Mash half an avocado and season with flaky sea salt, black pepper, and fresh lemon juice. Toast two ½-inch-thick slices of Jewish-Style Rye with Caraway (page 107). Spread 3 tablespoons of the mash on one slice of the toast. Top with a few thin slices each of turkey and garden tomato, strips of cooked bacon, and a fistful of arugula. Spread the top slice of toast with Dijonnaise (recipe follows) and close up the sandwich. Slice in half or in quarters and enjoy!

DIJONNAISE
Makes a scant 1½ cups

1 cup mayonnaise
⅓ cup sour cream
2 tablespoons Dijon mustard

In a small bowl, whisk together the mayonnaise, sour cream, and mustard until nicely incorporated. It will keep, tightly covered in the refrigerator, for up to 3 weeks.

SLIDERS

As easy to make as they are to eat, these three-bite sandwiches are perfect for a snack or stacked up on a platter for a brunch party. Just multiply all the ingredients by the number of sandwiches you want to make.

SMOKED SALMON SLIDER

In a small bowl, mix 1 teaspoon chopped fresh dill with 3 tablespoons crème fraîche. Spread it on the bottom of a Brioche Bun (page 168) and top with 2 slices smoked salmon. Season with freshly ground black pepper, a pinch of finely grated lemon zest, and minced chives. Drizzle good-quality olive oil on the underside of the top of the bun, close up the sandwich, and enjoy.

EGG AND OLIVE SLIDER

Spread the bottom half of a Brioche Bun (page 168) with 1 to 2 tablespoons of Kalamata Olive Puree (page 288). Top with a slice of hard-boiled egg (from a hard-boiled egg sliced lengthwise into thirds). Season with freshly ground black pepper and top with baby spinach leaves. Drizzle some good-quality olive oil on the underside of the top of the bun, close up the sandwich, and eat!

GOAT CHEESE CROISSANT SANDWICH

Oven-roasted plum tomatoes are the sweet, glistening gems in this sandwich. Combine them with creamy, tangy goat cheese and a flaky, savory croissant, and you have perfection.

Slice open a croissant horizontally. On the bottom half, spread 2 tablespoons of softened goat cheese, then top with 3 or 4 roasted tomatoes (see page 245), and a small handful of baby spinach leaves. Drizzle good-quality olive oil over the spinach, and season with flaky salt and freshly ground black pepper. Close up the sandwich and enjoy!

HUMMUS TOAST

Roast more eggplant than you need for this delicious toast; if you have the eggplant on hand, this is an ideal straight-from-the-refrigerator lunch.

Drizzle olive oil all over a toasted slice of sourdough, then spread 3 tablespoons good-quality hummus over it. Season with salt. Arrange 3 or 4 slices Roasted Eggplant (recipe follows) over the hummus followed by a smear of Kalamata Olive Puree (recipe follows). Drizzle with more olive oil, season with freshly ground black pepper, shower with chopped parsley, and serve.

ROASTED EGGPLANT

Preheat the oven to 400°F. Line a sheet pan with parchment paper. Trim the ends off of the eggplant(s), then cut crosswise into ¼- to ½-inch-thick slabs and arrange on the lined pan. Poke all over with a fork, then drizzle olive oil over and season with salt and freshly ground black pepper. Roast until caramelized and meltingly tender, about 20 minutes.

KALAMATA OLIVE PUREE

In a food processor, put 2 cups drained, pitted olives and pulse until a chunky paste forms. Don't overprocess or you will wind up with olive soup. Add 1 tablespoon olive oil and pulse just until the paste becomes a puree. Season with freshly ground black pepper and stir in a splash of lemon juice. The puree will keep, covered tightly in the refrigerator, for 2 weeks. Makes 1 to 1½ cups puree.

BREAD, ONE DAY LATER

There is nothing like the taste of freshly baked bread, but day-old bread has its place in the preparation of certain classic dishes. Stratas, bostocks, bread puddings—they are all best made with bread that has lost a bit of its moisture, so that it can properly soak up the liquids that it sits in without becoming mushy.

PECAN TOASTS (BOSTOCK)

MAKES 4 TOASTS

This French pastry is a good use of day-old brioche; some might say it's a good reason for brioche to exist. Be sure to spread the almond cream only to within ¼ inch of the edge of the bread so that it doesn't overflow during baking. The candied pecans and cinnamon almond cream can be made a day in advance.

FOR THE CANDIED PECANS:

1 small egg white

2 tablespoons sugar

⅔ cup pecan pieces

FOR THE CINNAMON ALMOND CREAM:

1 cup almond flour

¼ cup all-purpose flour

Large pinch of ground cinnamon

Pinch of ground nutmeg

5 tablespoons unsalted butter, at room temperature

6 tablespoons sugar

1 large egg

FOR THE SOAKING CUSTARD:

1 cup half-and-half

2 tablespoons honey

2 large eggs

¾ teaspoon ground cinnamon

Pinch of kosher salt

FOR ASSEMBLY:

4 (1-inch-thick) slices Brioche Loaf (page 167)

½ cup good-quality berry jam

Maple syrup, for serving

1. MAKE THE CANDIED PECANS: Preheat the oven to 350°F. Line a baking sheet with parchment paper or a silicone baking mat.

2. In a medium bowl, mix together the egg white and sugar with a fork to form a paste. Add the pecan pieces and stir until they are thoroughly coated. Spread the coated nuts in a single layer on the prepared baking sheet and bake until they are golden brown, about 15 minutes.

3. Slide the parchment with the nuts on it off the baking sheet and onto a cooling rack. Leave the oven on. Line the baking sheet with another piece of parchment and set aside.

4. MAKE THE CINNAMON ALMOND CREAM: In a medium bowl, whisk together both flours, the cinnamon, and nutmeg.

5. In a stand mixer fitted with the paddle attachment, beat the butter and sugar on medium speed until just combined. With the mixer running, add the egg and continue mixing until thoroughly incorporated. Turn the mixer to low, add the flour mixture, and mix until there are no traces of dry particles in the cream. Set aside until ready to use.

RECIPE CONTINUES

6. MAKE THE SOAKING CUSTARD: In a small saucepan, combine ⅔ cup of the half-and-half and the honey and heat over medium heat just until the honey dissolves. In a medium bowl, combine the remaining ⅓ cup half-and-half, the eggs, cinnamon, and salt. Whisk in the honey mixture. Divide the soaking custard between two shallow 9 × 13-inch baking dishes.

7. TO ASSEMBLE: Set the brioche slices in the dishes in a single layer to soak, about 3 minutes per side. Lift the slices from the soaking custard one at a time, and gently squeeze the excess liquid from each. Place the slices in a single layer on the lined baking sheet. Spread the cinnamon almond cream on each slice to within about ¼ inch of the edges all around, dividing it evenly.

8. Spread 2 tablespoons jam over the cream on each slice. Sprinkle the candied pecans over the jam, dividing them equally among the slices.

9. Bake until the almond cream is deep golden and the bottoms of the brioche slices are dry, about 35 minutes. Transfer to a rack to cool. Serve warm with maple syrup.

ZUPPA DI PANE

Our director of retail operations, Rosella Albanese (see her profile, page 276), grew up eating this for breakfast, a concoction her Italian mother made in remembrance of growing up in a tiny village in the mountains of Calabria. Rosella remembers it this way: "My mother kept a bin of stale bread in the kitchen. In the morning, she would break it up into small pieces into a cereal bowl. Then she warmed up some milk with a teaspoon of sugar, watching it closely so as not to let it boil over, and added it to the bowl. Finally, she'd pour espresso over the bread pieces and serve it to me for breakfast. It started out crunchy, but as you worked your way to the bottom of the bowl, it became the most delicious mush."

STRATA

SERVES 8 TO 10

This is the ideal make-ahead breakfast or brunch; the sourdough pieces must soak overnight in the egg mixture in order to smoothly incorporate themselves. Before you begin this recipe, toss the cauliflower and shallot in a thin coat of olive oil and roast on separate sheet pans at 400°F until they are fork-tender.

4 cups day-old sourdough, cut into 1½-inch cubes

8 large eggs

2 cups whole milk

1 teaspoon coarse kosher salt

2 teaspoons freshly ground black pepper

1 tablespoon fresh thyme leaves

1 cup grated cheddar, Comté, or other easy-grating cheese

2 cups cauliflower florets, roasted

1 shallot (about the size of a small lemon), roasted and coarsely chopped

¼ pound cooked ham or turkey, diced

Neutral-flavored cooking spray

1. Arrange the bread in an even layer in a 9 × 13-inch baking dish. In a bowl, whisk to combine the eggs, milk, salt, pepper, and thyme until the mixture is pale yellow and smooth. Add the cheese, cauliflower, shallot, and ham to the liquid mixture, using the whisk to distribute them evenly and to break up any clumps of cheese.

2. Pour the mixture over the bread. Coat the dull side of a piece of aluminum foil large enough to cover the strata with neutral cooking spray. Cover the strata and chill overnight in the refrigerator.

3. Preheat the oven to 400°F. Place the dish on a rimmed baking sheet and bake, covered, 1½ hours. Uncover and bake until the strata is puffed and golden brown, 15 to 20 minutes more.

4. Transfer the pan to a wire rack and let the strata cool for 10 minutes (it will firm up a bit, making it easier to slice into) before serving.

CROQUE-MONSIEUR

SERVES 1

What is a French café without a croque-monsieur? We make ours open-faced, a thick slice of sourdough slicked with béchamel and piled high with smoky Black Forest ham and bubbling Comté. Bake this until the cheese is bubbling and the edges of the bread are dark and crispy.

Good-quality unsalted butter, at room temperature (about 65°F)

1 (1½-inch-thick) slice sourdough, preferably cut from the widest part of the bread

3 tablespoons Béchamel (recipe follows)

2 (⅛-inch-thick) slices baked ham

3 tablespoons grated Comté or cheddar cheese

Freshly ground black pepper

1. Preheat the oven to 350°F. Line a half-sheet pan with parchment paper.

2. Generously butter one side of the bread and place it, buttered-side down, on the sheet pan. Spread 2 tablespoons of the béchamel all over the bread, then top with the ham, folding it over as necessary to keep it from hanging over the bread. Drizzle the remaining 1 tablespoon béchamel over the ham (this helps the cheese stick). Scatter the cheese evenly to the edges of the bread. Season with pepper.

3. Bake until the cheese is completely melted and bubbling, 15 to 20 minutes. Serve immediately.

BÉCHAMEL

Makes about 1 cup

1 tablespoon plus 1 teaspoon unsalted butter
2½ tablespoons all-purpose flour
⅔ cup whole milk
1 tablespoon grated Comté or cheddar cheese
Pinch of kosher salt
Pinch of ground nutmeg

In a small saucepan, melt the butter over medium heat until foamy. Gradually whisk in the flour until a paste forms. Add 2 tablespoons of the milk, whisking constantly, to form a liquid base. Add the remaining milk and increase the heat to high. Bring the milk to a boil, whisking constantly, until the mixture is thick enough to coat the back of a spoon. Remove from the heat and whisk in the cheese, salt, and nutmeg. The béchamel will keep, cooled first and covered directly with plastic wrap (to prevent a skin from forming), for up to 5 days.

BREAD PUDDING

SERVES 8

Any day-old soft and/or enriched bread, such as croissants or brioche or even a mix of the two, will work here; baguettes and sourdough are not the best candidates.

Unsalted butter, for the pan

3 cups half-and-half

4 large eggs

½ cup granulated sugar

¼ cup fresh lemon juice

Pinch of kosher salt

Fat pinch of ground cinnamon

1 loaf day-old brioche or any soft bread, or 8 croissants, or a mix of both, cut into 1-inch chunks to make 8 to 10 cups

1 cup blueberries or equal volume of any fruit

2 tablespoons cane sugar, for sprinkling

Crème Anglaise (recipe follows), for serving

1. Preheat the oven to 325°F. Slick a 9 × 5-inch loaf pan with a thin coat of butter.

2. In a large bowl, whisk together the half-and-half, eggs, granulated sugar, lemon juice, salt, and cinnamon until thoroughly combined.

3. Add the bread pieces and blueberries to the bowl and submerge until the bread has softened, 5 to 10 minutes. Pour the mixture into the prepared pan. Sprinkle the cane sugar evenly over the top.

4. Bake until a cake tester inserted in the middle comes out clean, about 1 hour 20 minutes. Let cool until the pudding has set, about 30 minutes. Serve drizzled with crème anglaise.

CRÈME ANGLAISE

3 egg yolks

¼ cup sugar

1 cup half-and-half

¼ teaspoon vanilla extract

Pinch of kosher salt

In a medium bowl, whisk together the egg yolks and 2 tablespoons of the sugar until frothy. Set aside. Combine the half-and-half, remaining 2 tablespoons sugar, the vanilla, and salt in a heavy-bottomed saucepan and heat over medium heat until it comes to a simmer. Remove from the heat. Whisking constantly, pour half of this mixture into the eggs. Slowly pour the egg and milk mixture back into the saucepan, whisking constantly. Stir over low heat until the mixture thickens; it will leave a path on the back of a spoon when you draw your finger across it, about 5 minutes. Pour through a strainer into a bowl. Cover with plastic wrap and chill.

RECIPES from RESTAUR PAIN D'AV

ANT
IGNON

During the winter of 2008, I was at the Cottbus Film Festival in Germany when I received a frantic call from Snežana. She was screaming at the top of her lungs and I couldn't understand what she was saying. "The bakery burned down, the bakery burned down." My knees buckled. "THERE WAS A FIRE IN THE BAKERY ON CAPE COD."

Around 3 or 4 a.m., when all the bakers and packers had already gone home and the drivers were in their trucks delivering bread, the electrical components on one of the ovens caught on fire. In no time the roof was aflame and quickly collapsed. Anything that didn't catch on fire was destroyed by the water used to put the fire out. In a last-ditch effort, Toma rummaged through the rubble to see if anything could be salvaged—ingredients, packaging materials, small equipment—but there was nothing left.

He worked frantically with Bane and Tole to move a small crew of bakers, packers, and drivers from Cape Cod to New York City the next day. Tole rented five hotel rooms in a motel near the bakery and waited for the crew from the Cape to arrive. We found an opening of about four hours before our New York baking would begin, and the day after the fire, the bread was made in New York and delivered to customers in Boston and on the Cape on time.

Our customers showed us unprecedented loyalty and support, as did the group of workers who came from Cape Cod. Not only did they come to work in New York without any notice and without time to pack properly, but as the days went by, they soon realized that they would be away from their homes and families for the next six months—and they never complained about it.

Losing the bakery was gut-wrenching, but we had no choice but to move forward. And we did so, with even bigger dreams. Six months after the fire, the new Pain d'Avignon opened just a few hundred yards from the old one. The new space was much bigger and nicer, and so Vojin decided to dedicate part of it to a proper restaurant. This wouldn't have been possible without Vojin's wife, Diana, who became a crucial member of the Cape Cod operation. Besides the fact that she was great with numbers, rational, and extremely hard-working, she brought a desperately needed maturity to the adolescent boys' club. With Diana as his anchor along with his charming right-hand man, super Mario Mariani, who is by far the best host that Cape Cod has ever seen, Vojin envisioned a sophisticated yet relaxed, warm, and welcoming restaurant; it has become a favorite of many local customers as well as restaurant fans from all over the country. He created a beautiful space—call it industrial warehouse meets European brasserie. The menu is fundamentally French, but it is heavily influenced by Vojin's own obsession with Mediterranean flavors and colors. He is a passionate fisherman, boater, and scuba diver who loves getting the freshest seafood on the Cape—from Wellfleet oysters to tuna (500 pounds!) he catches himself. The black-and-white interior is punctuated by a bright red bar, which has become synonymous with the restaurant. A huge window in the dining room allows customers to watch the bakers baking. It was our dream of bread theater writ large.

WILD MUSHROOM BRUSCHETTA

MAKES 1 BRUSCHETTA

This makes one 5-inch square bruschetta—perhaps large enough to share.

2 tablespoons olive oil, plus more for drizzling

1 cup wild mushrooms (oyster, chanterelle, hen-of-the-woods), chopped

2 cloves garlic, finely chopped

Kosher salt and freshly ground black pepper

1 tablespoon chopped fresh parsley

1 tablespoon unsalted butter, at room temperature

1 (5-inch) square piece "Focazza" (page 143), grilled or toasted, or 1½-inch-thick slice of sourdough, grilled or toasted

2 ounces burrata

Microgreens, for garnish

In a skillet, heat the oil over medium heat just until it shimmers. Add the mushrooms and sauté until they soften and release their liquid, 2 to 3 minutes. Add the garlic, season with salt and pepper to taste, and sauté until the garlic softens and is fragrant, about 3 minutes. Remove the pan from the heat and stir in the parsley and butter until the butter melts and the parsley is nicely distributed. Place the focazza in the center of a plate and spoon the mushroom mixture over it. Top with the burrata, drizzle with olive oil, and garnish with microgreens. Serve warm.

PANZANELLA SALAD

SERVES 6 TO 8

This is a summer/early fall must, when tomatoes are at their peak. Their juices seep into the bread cubes, giving the bread the perfect texture.

6 cups 1½-inch cubes Ciabatta (page 139) or Traditional Sourdough (page 101)

2½ pounds mixed heirloom tomatoes, cut into bite-sized pieces

20 large fresh basil leaves, coarsely chopped, plus a few whole leaves for garnish

10 cloves garlic, thinly sliced

5 tablespoons capers, drained

1 English (hothouse) cucumber, peeled, halved lengthwise, seeded, and sliced crosswise into ½-inch-thick slices

1 large red onion, halved and thinly sliced

1 cup extra-virgin olive oil

¼ cup champagne vinegar

Kosher salt and freshly ground black pepper

1. Preheat the oven to 350°F.

2. Arrange the bread cubes on two baking sheets and bake until golden, about 10 minutes. Set aside to cool.

3. In a large bowl, combine the tomatoes, basil, garlic, capers, cucumber, onion, olive oil, and vinegar. Season liberally with salt and pepper and gently toss. Let the mixture sit for at least 30 minutes to allow the flavors to marry.

4. Fold the toasted bread cubes into the mixture, taste for seasoning, and let sit for 5 minutes more. Serve on a large platter or individual plates, garnished with the whole basil leaves.

TRUFFLED EGG TARTINE

MAKES 4 TARTINES

The addition of truffle oil turns a perfectly good open-faced sandwich into something else altogether. Take care not to overtoast the bread here—a golden brown is what you are going for.

5 large eggs, hard-boiled

½ cup mayonnaise

1 tablespoon chopped fresh parsley

1 tablespoon truffle oil

Kosher salt and freshly ground black pepper

4 (½-inch-thick) slices Traditional Sourdough (page 101), toasted to just golden

Baby arugula, for garnish

1. Grate the eggs on the large holes of a box grater. Alternatively, chop them into ½-inch pieces. Place in a bowl and add the mayonnaise, parsley, and truffle oil and gently fold together. Season with salt and pepper to taste.

2. Top the bread slices with the egg mixture, spreading it out to the edges. Cut each slice in half crosswise, garnish with arugula, and serve.

PAIN PERDU SALÉ

MAKES 1

This triple-decker ham and cheese sandwich is dipped in a nutmeg-spiced egg mixture and cooked to a toasty golden brown, much like a classic Monte Cristo. Serve warm with a simple salad.

⅓ cup whole milk

1 large egg

Pinch of grated nutmeg

Kosher salt and freshly ground black pepper

2 tablespoons unsalted butter, softened

1 tablespoon Dijon mustard

3 slices White French Pullman (page 144)

2 slices smoked ham

2 slices Gruyère cheese

1. In a wide shallow bowl, whisk together the milk, egg, nutmeg, and salt and pepper to taste. Set aside.

2. In a small bowl, whisk together 1 tablespoon of the butter and the mustard.

3. Brush 2 slices of the bread with 1½ teaspoons of the butter-mustard mixture. Put 1 slice of the ham and 1 slice of the Gruyère on one of these slices. Top with the second slice, buttered-side down. Spread the top of this slice of bread with 1½ teaspoons of the butter-mustard mixture and lay the remaining ham and cheese on it. Spread the remaining piece of bread with the remaining butter-mustard mixture and close up the sandwich with it, buttered-side down. Place a heavy pot or cutting board on top of the sandwich for 30 seconds or so to press it together (this helps to keep it together when you dip it in the egg mixture).

4. In a heavy-bottomed skillet, melt the remaining 1 tablespoon butter over medium-high heat. Dip the sandwich in the egg mixture, lingering over the bowl to let the excess drip off. Place in the skillet and cook until the bottom is golden brown, about 5 minutes. Flip the sandwich and cook until the bottom is that same golden brown. Remove to a cutting board and slice on the diagonal. Serve warm.

SHRIMP PROVENÇALE

SERVES 4

Pernod is an anise-flavored aperitif sipped everywhere in the South of France. It is poured over a few ice cubes and mixed with a bit of water, with more water served on the side in a small pitcher. Pastis, another anise-flavored liqueur, is fine to use here, too. At the restaurant, we leave the heads and tails on the shrimp, as both are full of flavor. Of course, it is fine to peel them entirely, if desired.

16 head-on shrimp (8/12 count), peeled and deveined, heads and tails left on

Kosher salt and freshly ground black pepper

4 tablespoons extra-virgin olive oil

4 cloves garlic, minced

¼ cup Pernod

2 tablespoons chopped fresh parsley

2 plum tomatoes, seeded and finely diced

4 tablespoons (½ stick) unsalted butter

2 or 3 slices Classic Baguette (page 147), grilled or toasted

Season the shrimp with salt and pepper. In a large skillet, heat 2 tablespoons of the oil over medium-high heat until shimmering. Add the shrimp and sauté, turning once, until they are lightly browned and barely opaque, 2 to 3 minutes. Add the remaining 2 tablespoons olive oil along with the garlic and sauté for 30 seconds. Carefully add the Pernod and leave on the heat until it evaporates. Using a slotted spoon, remove the shrimp to a plate. Add the parsley, tomatoes, and butter to the pan and cook until the butter has melted and the tomatoes release their liquid. Bring the mixture to a simmer. Return the shrimp to the pan and cook until heated through. Serve warm with the bread.

ROASTED BRUSSELS SPROUTS WITH SPICED CHICKPEAS

SERVES 6 TO 8

The combination of flavors in this hearty side dish, seasoned with warm and smoky spices, is everything you crave in a cold-weather salad. If you can't find black chickpeas, yellow ones will do just fine here.

4 tablespoons olive oil

1 medium red onion, diced

2 cloves garlic, minced

1 tablespoon grated fresh ginger

1 teaspoon ground coriander

1 teaspoon ground cumin

1 teaspoon smoked paprika

¼ teaspoon ground cinnamon

Pinch of cayenne pepper

1 cup black chickpeas, soaked overnight and drained

½ cup golden raisins, soaked in hot water for 1 hour and drained

Kosher salt and freshly ground black pepper

2 quarts vegetable stock

¾ pound Brussels sprouts, cleaned and quartered

1 teaspoon minced shallots

2 tablespoons pecans, toasted and roughly chopped

Grilled Traditional Sourdough slices (page 101), for serving

1. In a 5-quart pot, heat 2 tablespoons of the olive oil over medium-high heat. Add the onion, garlic, and ginger and cook, stirring, until the onions soften and the mixture is fragrant, about 5 minutes.

2. Add the coriander, cumin, smoked paprika, cinnamon, and cayenne and cook until fragrant, about 2 minutes. Add the chickpeas and raisins and season with salt and pepper to taste. Stir to coat in the seasonings. Add the stock and bring to a boil. Reduce to a simmer, cover, and cook until the chickpeas split when pressed against the side of the pot with a spoon, about 3 hours. Add more stock to the pot if the mixture becomes dry; it shouldn't be soupy.

3. Meanwhile, preheat the oven to 350°F.

4. In a large bowl, toss the Brussels sprouts with the remaining 2 tablespoons olive oil and season with salt and pepper. Spread the Brussels sprouts in a single layer on a sheet pan and roast until they give when pierced with a fork, 20 to 30 minutes.

5. Put the Brussels sprouts on a serving platter and top with the chickpea mixture. Scatter the shallots and pecans all over. Taste and season with more salt and pepper if desired. Serve warm or at room temperature with sourdough.

FRENCH DIP À LA PAIN D'AVIGNON

SERVES 4

The French actually had nothing to do with the creation of the French dip, which is an American sandwich of shredded chuck roast and melted Swiss cheese on a baguette that gets "dipped" in beef broth. Ours is actually a bit of a higher-brow hybrid: thinly sliced filet mignon topped with a silken blue cheese sauce and topped with crispy fried onions.

FOR THE ONION RINGS:

1 cup all-purpose flour

½ cup finely ground cornmeal

2 tablespoons cornstarch

½ cup buttermilk

1 quart peanut oil

1 large onion, thinly sliced into rings, separated

Kosher salt

FOR THE SANDWICH:

1 pound filet mignon

Kosher salt and freshly ground black pepper

2 teaspoons olive oil

¾ cup heavy cream, or more if needed

6 ounces blue cheese

¼ teaspoon ground white pepper

2 cups beef broth or stock

4 (1½-inch-thick) slices Brioche Loaf (page 167), toasted

1. MAKE THE ONION RINGS: Whisk together the flour, cornmeal, and cornstarch in a shallow bowl. Pour the buttermilk into a second shallow bowl. Heat the oil over high heat in a deep, narrow heavy-bottomed pot until shimmering. Working in batches, toss the onion rings in the flour, then dip in the buttermilk. Let any excess buttermilk drip off the onions, then dredge a second time in the flour. Shake off the excess flour and fry until golden, using tongs to gently separate the onions. Transfer to paper towels to drain and season with salt.

2. MAKE THE SANDWICH: Season the filet all over with salt and pepper. In a large skillet, heat the oil over medium-high heat until it is hot but not smoking. Slide the filet into the pan and sear for 2 minutes per side, turning once, or until an instant-read thermometer reads 135°F for medium-rare. Remove to a cutting board and let rest.

3. In a small heavy-bottomed saucepan, heat the heavy cream over medium heat until it thickens slightly, 2 to 3 minutes. Whisk in the blue cheese and white pepper, cover, and cook for 5 minutes. Transfer the mixture to a blender and blend until smooth, adding a bit more cream if too thick.

4. Thinly slice the filet across the grain. In a saucepan, warm up the beef broth, then add the slices of filet to heat through. Set the brioche toasts on a plate. Scoop the filet out of the broth and set on the toasts, then spoon the blue cheese sauce over. Top with the onion rings and serve with the beef broth for dipping.

PDA BURGER

MAKES 4 BURGERS

This is one of the restaurant's classics, a mix of ground beef chuck and ground short ribs in a ratio of 80% lean meat to 20% full-fat meat, a proportion we find essential for juicy burgers.

1 pound ground beef chuck

1 pound ground short ribs

1½ teaspoons kosher salt

1½ teaspoons freshly ground black pepper

4 slices cheddar cheese

4 Brioche Buns (page 168), split and toasted

8 slices bacon, cooked to crisp

1 avocado, sliced

1 large tomato, thinly sliced

4 leaves Bibb lettuce

Aioli of your choice

1. In a medium bowl, combine the ground meats. Add the salt and pepper and gently mix with your hands, taking care not to overmix. Divide the meat into 4 equal portions, then loosely shape into patties. Make a small indentation in the center of each to prevent the burger from bulging during grilling.

2. Heat a grill pan over high heat until hot. Sear the patties for 3 to 4 minutes per side. About 1 minute before the burgers are done, lay a slice of cheddar on top of each.

3. To assemble each burger, arrange a patty on the bottom of a bun. Top with the bacon, avocado, tomato, lettuce, and aioli.

PAIN PERDU SUCRÉ

MAKES 6 SLICES

A hint of fragrant orange blossom water flavors this classic French toast, ideally made with day-old brioche.

4 large eggs

1⅔ cups whole milk

1 tablespoon orange blossom water

⅓ cup granulated sugar

3 tablespoons unsalted butter

6 (½-inch-thick) slices Brioche Loaf (page 167)

Powdered sugar, for sprinkling

Maple syrup, warmed, for serving

1. In a medium bowl, whisk together the eggs, milk, orange blossom water, and granulated sugar and set aside.

2. In a large skillet, melt 1 tablespoon of the butter over medium heat. Working with 2 slices of brioche at a time, dip them individually in the egg mixture and let the excess drip back into the bowl. Put the bread side by side in the pan and cook until the bottoms are golden brown, about 2 minutes, then flip and cook the other side in the same way. Transfer to a warm plate and continue with the remaining brioche slices and butter.

3. Arrange on a plate and tap the powdered sugar through a fine-mesh sieve all over the slices. Serve with maple syrup.

Gilles Heron,
Pain d'Avignon CEO

As for the future, it is not a question of foreseeing it, but of making it possible.
—**ANTOINE DE SAINT-EXUPÉRY**

It is through these words that my father, Guy, a career soldier in the French army, and my mother, Madeleine, an administrative agent, educated me and my older brother, Olivier. Together, they were ideal parents: She made room for us to dream, and he cultivated in us a duty best described by a favorite line shared with his soldiers: "A man must face up to his responsibilities, whatever his choices."

We moved every three years as army kids, and along the way discovered the most beautiful regions of France. A strict education, therefore, but a dreamy childhood. We may have had passing friendships, but so many of them remained indelibly fixed in our imaginations. One of them is what brought me to America.

At the age of twenty-one, I went to Atlanta, Georgia, in search of employment. Although my English was almost nonexistent, my youth and total carefree attitude helped me create friendships that, fifteen years later, still exist. I eventually returned to France to deepen my technical knowledge and acquire new professional credentials, all the while continuing to travel in France. Ultimately, I settled on an island in the Indian Ocean to create my own companies.

In 2003, a professional encounter quickly turned into an adventure that, in retrospect, marked a milestone in my life. Roland Feuillas, a farmer, miller, and baker living in the Hautes-Corbières, in the heart of the Cathar Valley, a region of Occitania, passed on to me his knowledge and love for ancient wheat, which, loosely defined, is natural wheat, not genetically modified and cultivated in a benevolent environment. It is used in a bread-making process that includes long fermentation, in which enzymes break down the gluten to make the bread more digestible.

It is bread that combines the know-how of the farmer with the art of the baker, and it became a passion that I wished to humbly pass on to others.

Ancient wheat, bread, transmission, brotherhood—these are words that now have meaning in my life. The desire to show others the way of ancient grains has fermented over the years to become a serious pursuit here in the US, where I am developing ancient wheat breads. And that is how we came to know our friends at Pain d'Avignon.

I had been living for more than nine years on the island of Réunion in the Indian Ocean with Anaïs, my lovely wife, and our young boys, Lucas and Thibault. We had a part of our family, our businesses, our friends, the Hermitage Lagoon, the Fournaise Volcano, the tropical climate—and somehow our habits, our routines. But the future becomes possible only if we provoke it. The anxiety of starting a new chapter in our lives across an ocean was frightening, but the discoveries we were about to make persuaded us to take Roland's vision to America. It is a choice that we do not regret, whatever the future may bring.

There has been laughter and tears, joy and fear—and infinite fulfillment. Being immigrants allows us to share unforgettable experiences with our children, family, and friends. It has allowed us to redefine our priorities and it has brought us all so much joy. We hope it never ends.

EQUIPMENT LIST

SPRAY BOTTLE

A small one comes in handy for spraying the surface of the Seven-Grain (page 108) before rolling it around in raw oats.

DIGITAL KITCHEN SCALE

All of the bread and pastry recipes in this book are written in metric weights for the simple reason that weighing ingredients results in greater accuracy. A digital scale with metric measures to within one-tenth of a gram is ideal.

INSTANT-READ DIGITAL THERMOMETER

Practiced bread bakers may be able to determine water temperature by feel, but the rest of us should remove that variable by using an instant-read digital thermometer. They can run anywhere from $12 to $100; for bread-baking purposes, you need only a very basic model. Choose one that is straightforward and easy to use.

MIXING BOWLS

You'll need one 6-quart bowl for mixing and fermenting the dough and two 3-quart bowls for proofing loaves. I find 6-quart mixing bowls—anywhere from 18 to 24 inches across—are ideal for mixing the dough. When combining flour, water, and other ingredients, you want the bowl to be nice and roomy, wider than it is deep. Stainless-steel restaurant bowls (sold at any kitchen or restaurant supply store) are lightweight, easy to wash, and nest nicely should space be an issue. For proofing doughs, we use specialized baskets (see Proofing Baskets, opposite), but it is not necessary to buy these. Using 3-quart mixing bowls lined with a kitchen towel to proof the loaves makes it easy to transfer the dough from the proofing bowl to the hot pan without deflating or disturbing the dough too much.

LIDDED 1-QUART AND 2-QUART TRANSPARENT CONTAINERS

You want to watch your starter transform from a mass of dough into a loose, gurgling starter, so it's best to use a clear container with a lid for sealing it up.

LARGE CUTTING BOARD

At the bakery, we rest pre-shaped doughs on 16 × 24-inch wood boards. A large cutting board serves the same purpose. Why not just rest the dough on the countertop where the dough is shaped? A moveable surface comes in handy for a couple of reasons: If workspace is at a premium or if your kitchen is too warm (or too cool) or there's a draft, you can situate the board elsewhere.

BOWL SCRAPER AND BENCH SCRAPER

Sometimes called a dough spatula, a bowl scraper is rounded on one side and is an inexpensive and indispensable kitchen tool. Not only is it used to scrape away every last bit of dough as well as loosen bulk fermented dough from the bowl, but it is ideal for scraping sticky dough off of your hands.

A bench scraper has a fairly sharp straight blade edge that makes it an excellent tool for dividing doughs. It is essential for pre-shaping and shaping doughs, too. Of course, it is also meant to do what its name suggests, scrape down your workbench, or work surface.

KITCHEN TOWELS

Fermenting dough needs to be covered as it proofs. Natural-fiber dish towels—linen or cotton—allow the dough to breathe as it ferments. Flour-sack towels, in particular, are inexpensive and do the job nicely.

PROOFING BASKETS

In the bakery, we use linen-lined willow baskets, known as bannetons, for proofing our breads. These help to maintain the loaves' shape as they proof. They come in several sizes and materials, including the wicker we use as well as plastic. For 1-pound loaves, we use 8-inch baskets, unlined. And of course, you can just use a 3-quart mixing bowl lined with a kitchen towel.

COUCHE

A piece of heavy flax linen that is uncoated and unbleached, and is used to support baguettes during the proofing stage.

FLIPPING BOARD

This is a rectangular, thin piece of wood, generally 27½ inches long × 4 inches wide, that is used to transfer baguettes from the couche after proofing to the parchment paper for baking. They are available at baking supply stores and at www.tmbbaking.com. In a pinch, you can cut a piece of cardboard in the dimensions above to use as a flipping board.

DUTCH OVEN, CAST-IRON COMBO COOKER, OR A CHALLENGER BREAD PAN

A successful loaf of bread requires a sealed environment, steam, and even heat during the baking stage. At the bakery, we use professional deck ovens equipped with steam injectors to that end. The simplest way to best approximate this environment is by using a 4½-quart enameled cast-iron Dutch oven such as Le Creuset, or a 3.2-quart cast-iron combo cooker from Lodge (lodgecastiron.com). Either yields an admirable loaf, its sealed chambers keeping in the steam produced by the bread, which is essential for a predictable rise and good crust. You can bake long loaves in a Challenger bread pan (challengerbreadware.com) or on a baking stone.

HALF-SHEET PANS

You should have at least a pair of 13 × 18-inch half-sheet pans. These rimmed pans are essential for baking some of the brioche recipes, viennoiseries, scones, and cookies. Because they stack nicely and are easy to store, it doesn't hurt to have three or four (see Arlettes, page 230); they come in handy for setting proofing bowls on and using as a carrier for loose mixtures like Strata (page 298) when transferring to the oven.

LAME OR SINGLE-EDGE RAZOR BLADE

To score a loaf of bread, you need a very thin, sharp blade. Scores, or cuts, are essential for allowing the loaf to expand properly as it bakes. Professionals use a lame, a removable blade attached to a metal handle. You will find many variations available—wood-handled, fixed blade, etc.; just be sure the blade is thin and very sharp, otherwise the dough will tear. A single-edge razor blade or X-Acto blade will work in a pinch.

BAKING STONE

There are dozens of different baking stones on the market. At home we use a 14 × 16-inch cordierite stone, which isn't too heavy and very efficiently absorbs the oven's heat and transfers it to the bread.

ACKNOWLEDGMENTS

THANK YOU

To Megan Newman, vice president and publisher, and Lucia Watson, executive editor of Penguin Random House. No words can express our gratitude for the trust and support you extended from that very first afternoon meeting. Thank you from the bottom of our hearts.

To Kathleen Hackett. She said, "You talk and I will write." But sometime into the process I realized that I was mistaking my cowriter for the shrink I never had. She said, "Don't worry; you never know, maybe we will find something we could use later on." Maybe we did, but from the notes she took we could publish another three books. On arts, on politics, on parenthood. On friendship.

To Sharon Bowers, book agent nonpareil, who was always there, available day and night regardless of time zone, when I felt lost and paralyzed by the approaching deadlines. She still is.

To Ed Anderson, who shot the entire book during a single week in February 2021, both in New York City and on Cape Cod, where he had the additional challenge of photographing around masked faces. All the breads photographed were baked for our regular customers and were sent out the next morning for delivery. The breads—even those we weren't entirely happy with—became objects of art through the lens of Ed's camera and with the help of stylist Maeve Sheridan.

To David Polonsky. In 2008, I was casting around for funding to produce my first feature film. That same year, an amazing animated film called *Waltz with Bashir* came out, art directed and illustrated by David. I thought that if I ever made a film about the bakery, the pitch would be a combination of *Waltz with Bashir* and *Big Night.* Almost ten years later, as I began writing this book, I was reminded of this brilliant Israeli artist's work and reached out to him. David did not hesitate to accept the job of illustrating our story. "I love bread, I love friendship, I know immigration, I know war," he said. I will be forever humbled.

To our friends at Mucca Design, Matteo, Andrea, María, and Yoon, whose branding talents so perfectly capture the spirit of Pain d'Avignon. You continuously amaze us. Another great artist, Jeffrey Fisher, playfully captured who we are and what we are trying to do every day in the illustrations throughout the book.

To our talented book designer, Ashley Tucker, who elegantly brought illustration, photography, and text together on these pages.

To Francoise Ip, Pain d'Avignon's pastry chef, who worked together with Kathleen on the pastry recipes. And to Rosella Albanese, for collaborating on the recipes for Café d'Avignon. Thank you to Chef Christophe Gest on Cape Cod, who supplied us with Restaurant Pain d'Avignon's recipes. And a special thank-you to Diego Cubas for helping me with the bread-making process shots. A special thank-you to Lauren Holden, Nora Kohnhorst, Megan Meo, and Maria Wisdom for putting the recipes to the test.

To Mario Carbone, for taking the time during his extremely busy schedule to be our de facto first reader and write the foreword. His words make us hopeful that this book is a celebration of not only bread but the immigrant experience and of baking with purpose.

To my daughter, Nika, who was my Cyrano de Bergerac, and who helped me write down the sentences that were often stuck in my head. Knowing and understanding me so well, she articulated the thoughts I was not able to express myself. And to Snežana, who was patient enough to listen to the same chapters over and over again, all the while encouraging me to keep going.

To all of our employees both in New York and on Cape Cod. Thank you for the last three decades. Without you we would not exist. Literally.

INDEX

Note: Page numbers in *italic* indicate photos.

MASTERS OF THE PDA OVENS:
Atilano Reyes and Teofilo Rincon
have baked over **SIXTY MILLION**
pieces of **BREAD** and **PASTRIES**
over the last **TWENTY YEARS.**